SUPPLY CHAIN
LOGISTICS

Mid-Level Technical Knowledge for Frontline Workers

INDUSTRY 4.0 EDITION

Leo Reddy

Foreword by Gary Forger

This product was initially funded under a 2007 grant by the U.S. Department of Labor's Employment and Training Administration. The information contained in this product was created by a grantee organization and does not necessarily reflect the official position of the U.S. Department of Labor. All references to non-governmental companies or organizations, their services, products, or resources are offered for informational purposes and should not be construed as an endorsement by the Department of Labor. This product is copyrighted by the institution that created it and is intended for individual organizational, non-commercial use only.

Foreword to the 4.0 Edition of CLT

By Gary Forger

By now, you know a whole lot more than you once did about what makes warehouses and distribution centers run 24/7. You are probably already a Certified Logistics Associate (CLA). And you may have already spent some time working in a warehouse too. Congratulations. You're on a great path.

Now it's time for that next step known as CLT or Certified Logistics Technician. This is the refreshed edition of the original textbook to get you to that next stage known as the *4.0 Edition of Supply Chain Logistics: Mid-Level Technical Knowledge.*

This book has already been beneficial to the more than 40,000 people who have received their CLT certificate. The combination of your CLA and CLT certificates forms the foundation for a long, rewarding career in supply chain logistics.

And, yes, you should be looking at this as a career, not just a job. Not only is the money good, but the work is rewarding too. In our economy, people understand and appreciate supply chains that work as they are supposed to and in a timely manner. We've all been disappointed or worse by supply chains. Worse yet, you've probably had it happen more than once.

Now is your chance to have a direct impact on how supply chains work. This book is focused on many key processes and practices that make it possible to manage the flow of inventory from the receiving door to the shipping dock of a distribution center. Key areas here include receiving, storage and order processing as well as packaging and shipment.

You will also learn about many of the key tools that make managing that inventory possible from manual and automated storage equipment to advanced information systems that track and dispatch inventory and orders. It's all about control that ensures the right inventory is in the right place at the right time for the right customer. That's the ultimate definition of a successful supply chain.

And as you already know, not everything in the supply chain happens within the four walls of the warehouse. There's also a complex network of transportation modes that move those orders that you've just filled on to their destination.

Did you know that over-the-road trucks move 70% of the nation's freight by weight and travel more than 300 billion miles annually?

Or that a cargo plane (there are about 900 in the U.S.) holds as much as roughly five trucks.

Did you know that the entire U.S. rail network is more than 155,000 miles long?

Or that the seaborne international shipping industry moves about 90% of the world's goods on more than 500,000 merchant ships.

Clearly, the supply chain lives on a world stage, and you can too. But most important, your supply chain logistics career moves to the next level when you turn this page.

Notes

Acknowledgements

The preparation of this primer was originally supported by a U.S. Department of Labor (USDOL) grant to the North Central Texas Workforce Development Board. Under this grant, the Manufacturing Skill Standards Council (MSSC) was contracted in July 2007 to develop a certification program for front-line workers in supply chain logistics. The Department placed this grant under the "advanced manufacturing" section of its High Growth Jobs Initiative program. MSSC is a national leader in developing standards-based training, assessment and certification programs for the core competencies of front-line industrial workers.

This program is analogous to the one that MSSC has developed since the National Skill Standards Board officially recognized MSSC's industry-led, nationally validated foundational standards for production support workers in 2001. Covering all sectors of manufacturing, this program leads to the well-established Certified Production Technician (CPT) certification.

As with CPT, the CLT certification program for supply chain logistics includes standards, assessments and credentials, supported by courses, textbooks, teacher certification training, a registry and computer-based learning technologies.

The CLT certification program was publicly announced at a special event, "Training and Certifying the Workforce of the Future," at the ProMat 2009 International Logistics Show in Chicago on January 14, 2009, supported by the Material Handling Industry of America (MHIA). Under the USDOL grant, teachers were trained in the North Texas area in February and March, 2009, with courses beginning for 250 trainees in April, 2009. A North Texas Advanced Manufacturing and Logistics Summit in Dallas, in March 2009, inaugurated this training and outreach to the logistics community in that large intermodal hub.

The preparation of the original primer, Supply Chain Logistics: Foundational Knowledge, was a team effort in every way. The MSSC would first like to thank the U.S. Department of Labor's Employment and Training Administration for funding the development of the CLT program and the grant project team, led by Kent Andersen, Natalie Johnson and Marcia Brown at the Workforce Solutions North Central Texas, and Drew Casani and Rick Askew at the Texas Manufacturing Assistance Center. Steve Boecking, Vice President, Hillwood Alliance Global Logistics Hub in Fort Worth, played a key role in recruiting the industry subject matter experts who wrote the initial CLT standards.

This text is organized and formatted around the industry-led standards for CLA. It is largely a compilation of materials written by leading authorities in this field aligned with the content of those standards. Leo Reddy and Rebekah Hutton at MSSC conducted the research, prepared the initial drafts for expert review and edited the text. John Rauschenberger, Ph.D., edited the third edition. Allan Howie, Director of Continuing Education at the Material Handling Industry, was an important source of documentation and served as one of the key reviewers.

ACKNOWLEDGEMENTS

This Industry 4.0 version is far more than a routine update. To ensure that we were keeping pace with the increasingly rapid infusion of digital Industry 4.0 technologies into the distribution-logistics industry, we added a set of nine emerging technologies to the standards with the assistance of subject matter experts led by Gary Forger. With years of experience in technology road mapping for MHI, Gary helped guide the process of integrating 4.0 technologies into the CLT standards and the textbook. This task included the re-drafting of much of the CLT text to reflect significant technological changes in the industry, including others beyond the scope of 4.0 technologies, to thoroughly revise this Fourth Edition.

Bruce Dickson, MSSC's Senior Director for Program Development, worked in tandem with Gary and with Opus Works, long-established provider of eLearning curriculum for MSSC's CLA/CLT training, to make the corresponding changes in the CLT on-line curriculum in partnership with Opus Works. Bruce also worked on revising the CLT assessment with Dr. Katherine Manley, a nationally known expert on industry assessment from Ferris State University and contractor to the National Occupational Competencies Testing Institute (NOCTI). Anne Gielczyk, Vice President of NOCTI Business Solutions coordinated the assessment revision process. Additional editorial support for the textbook and powerpoints were provided from Subject Matter Experts Joann M. Pfingston and Mark T. Van Meter of Preeminent Training Specialists, LLC who have supported MSSC throughout the years with their real world industry leading knowledge and training. We also want to recognize the fine professional work of Todd Mitchell, Owner of the Mitchell Creative Group, for very meticulous work on the edits, formatting and graphics on this Fourth Edition.

Table of Contents

CHAPTER 1

CHAPTER 1

Product Receiving

Overview of Chapter

The purpose of this chapter is to explain the overall process of and the role of front-line material handling workers in product receiving. The receipt of materials into a warehouse, distribution center, production facility or retail outlet is a coordinated activity that can affect accuracy throughout the life cycle of a product. Front-line workers are an important part of the receiving process in unloading, verifying load accuracy and completing paperwork.

Objectives

When you have completed this chapter, you will be able to do these things:

1. Describe activities essential to receiving.

2. Identify procedures for handling inbound trucks.

3. Describe conditions for unloading, including security requirements.

4. List and describe documents for standard receipt of materials.

5. Describe procedures for checking and reporting inbound materials during unloading.

6. Describe procedures for identifying and reporting overages, shortages or damages.

Essential Receiving Activities

Receiving is the collection of activities involved in the orderly receipt of all **materials** coming into a facility such as a warehouse or distribution center. This provides assurance that the quality and quantity of materials are as ordered. Materials are then disbursed to storage locations or to other organizational functions requiring them.

Receiving is a deceptively simple process. Traditionally, order picking and shipping have been considered the most labor-intensive activities in warehouse operations, and thus deserve more attention than receiving. However, receiving is a function that can affect a company's bottom line directly if errors are made. The receiving process itself also typically involves processes, procedures and documentation (paper or electronic) that can be complicated. In addition, receiving personnel also work with outside personnel such as drivers. For these reasons, many companies put their more experienced people in the receiving department.

This training focuses primarily on the material handling procedures used with loading and unloading trucks. However, many of the same principles can be applied to handling materials that travel by rail cars, cargo airplanes and ocean-going shipping containers.

Receiving Process

There are sequential steps involved in effective receipt of materials at a facility. Each company may handle these steps slightly differently. Not all are needed in every situation, but all may play a role in the receiving process. Here are some common steps:

- Inbound trucker phones a facility to get a delivery appointment and provides information about the materials

- Receiving department verifies the Advanced Ship Notice (ASN) and confirms it with information from the inbound trucker

- Truck arrives and is assigned to a specific receiving door

- Truck is safely secured at the dock

- Seal on truck container door(s) is inspected and broken in the presence of a carrier representative (usually the truck driver)

- Materials are inspected and either accepted or refused

- Materials are unloaded

- All unloaded materials are staged for count and final inspection

- Proper documentation is made of damaged, missing or incorrect materials

- Materials are positioned for storage in an assigned location

Did You Know?

Vendor Compliance Program

One way to improve efficiency and accuracy in the receiving process is to implement a vendor compliance program or issue vendor specification manuals to all suppliers.

Examples of the types of specifications given to vendors and suppliers include:

- Quality requirements (amount number of acceptable defects, performance characteristics of the inventory).

- Product specifications (versions, lots, value added requirements, case pack or unit dimension requirements).

- Pallet sizes and stacking (floor loaded, slip sheet, pallets, shrink wrapped, over-all dimension limits, weight restrictions, pallet sizes allowed, quality of pallets).

- Product packaging (how to group and label loose product, mixed pallets, full pallets, sealing specs, dunnage requirements).

- Carton sizes and types (reusable totes, corrugated, drums, weight and size limits, quality of material).

- Shipping requirements (who, how, when).

By limiting any nonconforming product and associated rework on receipt of inventory, product can be more readily available to fulfill orders. Receipt efficiency, accuracy, and inventory availability can also be improved.

CHAPTER 1

Procedures for Handling Inbound Trucks

Careful planning and checking

The receipt of materials must be carefully planned. In most large facilities, incoming materials are scheduled in advance so appropriate resources can be allocated to the activity. On arrival, a driver reports to the gatehouse. Staff checks documentation and directs the driver where to go, either directly to an unloading bay or to a parking area.

The container's doors may be sealed, particularly in the case of imported materials. Where this occurs, the seal number must be checked against those advised by the sender to determine whether or not the door was opened during transit. If so, there may be a possibility of loss of materials.

Receiving is usually allowed only on a scheduled basis. Every carrier makes an appointment and is assigned an unloading time. Most carriers appreciate the precision of a scheduled dock and will cooperate with any operation that insists upon establishing unloading appointments. However, unscheduled containers occasionally arrive and must be handled efficiently and effectively.

While scheduling has obvious advantages, it also represents an obligation. When a facility

promises to unload an inbound truck at a specific time, it can expect to be penalized in the form of detention costs if it fails to keep that appointment.

Running a scheduled dock requires the ability to measure and predict workflow to allow the facility to keep the timetable that is set. In most cases, detention charges can be avoided if the completion time is kept, even if unloading begins late.

For example, if an inbound truck is scheduled for unloading between 10:00 a.m. and 12:00 p.m., it is not likely that detention charges will be incurred as long as unloading is completed by 12:00 p.m., even if the unloading did not begin until 10:30 a.m.

Efficient management of yard and dock

The yard and accompanying dock area are a focal point of logistics efficiency. Careful planning and design are essential. The need for easy access by trucks and the increase in time-sensitive deliveries and shipments require that the yard be a safe and efficient place.

To speed truck and rail docking, the yard must be designed to accept a variety of sizes and types of vehicles. A bottleneck in the yard can defeat any efforts inside the facility to be efficient and productive. If arriving materials do not get in the door in an efficient manner, then a domino effect can slow the entire operation.

Correct conditions before unloading

Before unloading, a container must be safely secured. With a truck this means that the wheels are chocked or an available dock locking device has been engaged. This ensures that there is no danger of the trailer moving during unloading.

In many warehouses, a supervisor is responsible for confirming that these safety checks have been completed. However, the ultimate responsibility lies with the un-loader to be cautious and aware, and to follow all safety procedures. Railroad car docking requires similar steps.

Security on receiving docks is very important because of the high level of activity and the involvement of outside personnel. Most companies have strict procedures for managing outside drivers, and these policies must be carefully followed. If outside drivers become too familiar with receiving procedures and personnel, it can result in a serious security breach.

Standard Product Delivery Documents

When materials are received, the receiving department inspects them to ensure that the correct materials have been sent in the right quantity and that they have not been damaged in transit. Using its copy of the purchase order and the bill of lading supplied by the carrier, the receiving department then accepts or rejects the materials and writes up a receiving report noting any variance.

Provided the materials are in order and require no further inspection, they are sent to the correct department or placed into inventory. A copy of the receiving report is then sent to the purchasing department noting any variance or discrepancy from the purchase order.

Each receipt resulting from a purchase order requires its own documentation. The billing and payment cycle generates additional documentation. All of these documents must reference the controlling purchase and sales orders.

All mapping among the documents must be carefully traced so that both companies are certain that what was ordered was shipped,

Think About It

Bill of Lading

What is the difference between a carrier and a shipper?

A carrier is the company responsible for transporting (carrying) the materials from the seller to the customer. The shipper is the seller of the materials. Sometimes shippers have their own transportation fleets. In that case, the shipper and the carrier are one and the same.

What is a consignee?

Consignee is a legal term used in the transportation of materials. It usually refers to the customer. It may also indicate that the purchaser does not have full legal ownership until the materials are received and accepted, and/or payment is made in full.

CHAPTER 1

and that payment was made for what was received.

These are just the documents that flow between the companies. The number of documents required within each company can be much larger.

Following are the most common receiving documents.

Bill of Lading

There are two types of bills of lading—the straight bill of lading and the order bill of lading. The straight bill of lading is the most common. The order bill of lading is used as a means for the shipper to obtain payment for the materials from the customer.

The straight bill of lading is used in virtually all shipping transactions. It comes in two types: standard and short form. The only difference between the two is that the short form does not contain the contract terms and conditions on the reverse side.

The straight bill of lading serves three primary purposes:

- A receipt from the carrier to the shipper for the materials received for transportation

- A contract of carriage

- A presumption of title to the materials.

The bill of lading should contain at least the following information:

- Shipper's name and address

- The consignee's name and address

- A description of the materials offered for transport

- The gross weight of the shipment

- An indication of who pays the freight charges— the shipper, the consignee or a third-party

Carrier Freight Bill

The carrier freight bill is an invoice presented by the carrier to the shipper, the consignee or a referenced third-party as a demand for payment for services rendered.

Like the bill of lading, it is a standard document. It includes, at minimum: the name of the carrier, the carrier's reference number (pro number) and address, a description of the materials, the rate, the freight terms and the charges due.

These documents must be carefully checked. Carriers are not perfect and have been known to make mistakes in preparing invoices.

Delivery Receipt

The delivery receipt is a document issued by the carrier that the consignee signs as proof of receipt. It is also known as a proof of delivery. The delivery receipt contains essentially the same information as the freight bill and the bill of lading. The consignee signs and dates it upon receipt of the materials delivered. The carrier retains a copy and the consignee retains a copy.

If materials are damaged at the time of delivery, the nature and extent of the damage must be noted on the delivery receipt. If the extent of the damage cannot be fully determined, a general statement should be made, such as "10 boxes crushed— contents subject to further inspection". When possible, the truck driver should sign to acknowledge damages or shortages.

Air Waybill

The air waybill is the airfreight industry's equivalent of the trucking industry's bill of lading. It serves the same general purpose and contains essentially the same information. The forms vary from carrier to carrier, or forwarder to forwarder, but in general, all ask for the same information. At minimum, an air waybill includes:

- Name and address of the shipper

- Name and address of consignee

- Gross weight of the shipment

- Indication of the service level required next day, second day, etc.

- Who is responsible for the freight charges

Checking and Reporting Inbound Materials

When the seal on a truck's container doors is inspected and broken, the truck driver should be present and initial the inspection form to verify that the seal number conforms

Terms to Know

Air Waybill
A bill of lading for air transport that serves as a receipt for the shipper. It indicates that the carrier has accepted the goods listed, and obligates the carrier to carry the consignment to the airport of destination according to specified conditions.

Advanced ship Notice (ASN)
An electronic data interchange (EDI) notification of shipment of product.

Bill of Lading
A carrier's contract and receipt for goods that the carrier agrees to transport from one place to another and to deliver to a designated person. In case of loss, damage, or delay, the bill of lading is the basis for filing freight claims.

Carrier Freight Bill
An invoice presented by the carrier to the shipper, the consignee or a referenced third-party as a demand for payment for services rendered.

Consignee
The receiver of shipment of freight — the customer.

Delivery Receipt
A document issued by the carrier that the consignee signs as proof of receipt. It is also known as a proof of delivery.

CHAPTER 1

to the one listed on the advanced ship notice (ASN). Any exceptions should be noted at this time.

When the trailer or container doors are opened, there is an initial inspection to determine whether the load will be accepted or refused. Sometimes there is a quality test made at this point to verify that the materials on the inbound load meet the receiver's specifications. For example, one fast food chain runs a random test on the fat content of hamburger meat before unloading proceeds. If the test fails, the entire load is refused.

If the materials are accepted, the material handler must:

- Check the materials against the order and the bill of lading

- Check the quantities

- Check for damage and fill out damage reports, if necessary

- Inspect materials, if required

If further inspection of incoming materials is required, the materials are sent to quality control or held in receiving for inspection.

Precision scales are often used to prevent theft or product substitution. In some cases, the facility may require random physical inspections in which boxes are opened and checked manually.

Many loads contain unitized or palletized materials and loose or floor-loaded materials. Both unitized and floor-loaded materials must be counted and checked. In most cases, the entire load is held in a staging area for final inspection. If there is a buying department on site, the buyer may wish to examine the staged materials before they are put away. However, in most cases, the bill is signed and the truck released once a final count of the staged materials has been completed.

A final step before releasing the truck is to account for any damages, shortages or overages. Depending upon conditions negotiated between receiver and shipper, carrier damage may be immediately refused to a trucker (the materials are not unloaded), or it may be held for carrier inspection and recouping of costs. In either case, the number of damaged pieces on the load must be noted on the inbound bill of lading and acknowledged by a carrier representative, usually the truck driver. It is especially important to note shortages or overages when handling international shipments.

If materials are damaged, the receiving department will advise the purchasing department and hold the materials for further action. If the load is accepted with damaged materials, the damaged materials must be separated and stored to avoid further damage.

After materials are unloaded at the receiving dock, they are often placed in one or more

temporary locations or staging points before being eventually placed in storage. Regardless of whether materials have assigned (dedicated) or random (floating) storage locations, they should be placed in the correct location. Furthermore, it is important for locations to be entered quickly and accurately into the locator system.

Materials arriving at the loading dock also require some form of labeling so they can be easily identified as to type of material and in some cases, usage planned for the materials. Sometimes items are pre-labeled by the vendor as dictated by a shared numbering or bar coded system. Material handling personnel are often asked to label materials in a manner determined by the tracking system of their employer.

Terms to Know

Material Handler
An individual who moves and stages materials within the supply chain.

Materials
This is a broad term that includes other terms such as goods, cargo, freight, loads, products and merchandise, to name a few.

Proof of Delivery
A document signed as proof of receipt of material or goods. Also known as a POD.

Receiving
The function encompassing the physical receipt of material, the inspection of the shipment for conformance with the purchase order (quantity and damage), the identification and delivery to destination, and the preparation of receiving reports.

Staging Area
The location in a facility where materials are organized. Newly received items can be staged before being placed in a final storage destination or into another container for transport. Inventory items may also be staged before being organized into orders for container loading.

Unitization
The process of consolidating several units into a single, larger unit to reduce the total number of handling for all units combined.

Yard
The outdoor area around a dock. It can refer to a shipping yard, rail yard or truck yard.

Notes

CHAPTER 2

Product Storage

Overview of Chapter

The purpose of this chapter is to explain how products are stored. Front-line workers should understand the foundational concepts that affect where and how products are stored. There are many types of storage equipment and systems from simple floor stacking to highly advanced, automated storage and retrieval systems. This chapter will provide an overview of those types of storage and the equipment used for each.

Objectives

When you have completed this chapter, you will be able to do these things:

1. List methods for determining destination and direction of unloaded materials.

2. Identify key issues affecting how materials are stored.

3. List forms in which materials are stored.

4. List options for storage.

5. Describe a system for automated storage and retrieval.

Destination and Direction of Unloaded Products

Determination of Location

All materials arrive at a facility with a designated use in mind. They must be directed and tracked as they are unloaded. This is a basic part of the distribution process. Materials are sent for a purpose: storage, distribution or for use in the production process.

Materials are often unloaded and placed in a staging area near the loading dock. They remain there until the next location to which they are to be delivered is determined. As materials are removed from the loading dock area, they are taken to a designated location, be it storage, manufacturing, distribution or order-picking.

CHAPTER 2

The delivery locations for incoming materials must be clearly marked or designated, and the products or contents must be clearly labeled. Materials do not simply enter a storage facility to be left for an indefinite period of time. They often arrive just in time to be included in an order to a customer.

A numbering system assigned to these locations is necessary to add structure and logic to the movement of the materials within the facility. This numbering system is often referred to as an address system or locator system. Just as the post office delivers mail and packages to addresses, distribution workers must deliver to and retrieve items from an address or location in the facility.

The determination of the precise location for incoming materials is typically made by use of a warehouse management system (WMS), a software program that matches materials to a desired destination and tracks movement.

Key Issues Affecting How Materials are Stored

Several issues affect how materials are stored:

• Mass, measurement and space

• Volume, density and size

• Depth, containment and process

• Weight, configuration and delivery

Among these, volume, density and size have the greatest impact.

Volume. How material is stored depends largely on volume. Volume takes into account how much of any one kind of material is on hand in a given period of time (quantity) and how much material is retrieved for shipment within a given period of time (throughput or velocity).

Density. Large quantities of any one item being stored are likely to be stored as unit loads (on pallets or in similar large containers). Furthermore, the larger the quantity, the more desirable it is to store unit loads in high density storage arrangements. This results in less floor space dedicated to the aisles and reduces the size of the storage facility. In general, the greater the volume, the greater the desire for high density storage arrangements.

Density is especially important when easy, frequent access to materials is required because of high throughput. This chapter will introduce various types of storage equipment that allows for different levels of density.

Size. As a criterion, size matters. But it comes into play mainly when dealing with individual items. Except in special circumstances, pallets, containers and cartons have fairly standard dimensions.

To summarize: Volume (quantity of materials) dictates how materials are stored and impacts density (storage arrangements) if throughput (how much material is retrieved for shipment within a given period of time) is not impacted.

Forms in Which Materials are Stored

Materials are generally stored and shipped in the manner in which they first arrived at the doors of a facility. How things are stored, and their quantity for subsequent retrieval and shipment, depends on whether they are pallets, cases/cartons or individual items.

In general, large demands for materials call for unit load retrieval and shipment. As demands and orders decrease in size, the process moves towards the retrieval and shipment of cases and eventually to individual items handled one or more at a time.

Forms of storage are also related to the type of facility and material involved. For example:

• Materials moved from a manufacturing facility to a distribution center are likely to be moved and then stored, at least initially, as pallet loads.

• Materials from a grocery distribution center retrieved and shipped (e.g., cans of soup at local retail stores) are likely to be stored and handled within the facility as cases.

Storage equipment suitable for efficiently dealing with pallets, boxes, cases, totes and similar storage units must be available.

Terms to Know

Automated storage/retrieval system (AS/RS)
A high-density, rack inventory storage system with vehicles automatically loading and unloading the racks.

Cantilever rack
A specialized form of rack used for storing long items such as lumber or pipes.

Double-deep storage (also called deep-reach)
Rack that holds two units deep, one behind the other.

Drive-in/Drive-through rack
High-density storage system that allows units to be stored several deep. Fork-trucks can drive between and into racks to retrieve items.

High-density storage
Storage system which allows pallets to be stored more than one unit deep or high.

Kitting
The process through which individual items are grouped or packaged to create a single shipment.

Mobile sliding rack
Storage racks that sit on tracks so they can be moved to retrieve items. An aisle can be opened between any two rows to allow access.

CHAPTER 2

Bulk

Grouping of similar unit loads

To help in retrieval and to facilitate inventory control, large numbers of unit loads of the same SKU or same type of materials are usually stacked on the floor together. This is called bulk stacking.

Height of the building ceiling

In a facility with lower ceiling heights (e.g., three or less stacked pallet loads) floor stacking may be used instead of purchasing a rack, or stacking frame. In most facilities, floor space is at a premium. No storage devices other than the pallet or skid on which materials are unitized are needed. Important considerations in evaluating the use of bulk stacking are:

• The stackability of the material

• Possible damage to the materials by crushing

• Material rotation — how long the material will be in the location

A stacking frame is a device consisting of interlocking units that enables stacking of materials so that crushing does not occur. These can be used to offset the negative effects of bulk stacking but are expensive and somewhat clumsy to use. At the same time, stacking frames can be affixed to the deck of a pallet and can be disassembled and stored compactly when not in use. By addressing strength and stability of loads formed on pallets, stacking frames can be used to enable multilevel bulk stacking.

Rack

Bulk stacking is not an option for all materials. Some materials simply should not be placed on the floor. The logical alternative for storing such materials is a storage rack. This particular storage device is familiar to almost everyone. Every home improvement center, discount warehouse or "big box store" has row upon row of storage racks.

The storage rack is usually made of formed or structural steel. The size and gauge of the steel for a given rack system is determined largely by the capacity needed to house and support the stored materials.

In using selective pallet racks, pallets of materials are placed in openings in the storage rack and supported by load-supporting beams.

Selective pallet racks can be used for the following types of storage:

- **Standard single-deep** storage using a counterbalanced lift truck.

- **Narrow-aisle** storage using a narrow-aisle reach truck.

- **Deep-reach** greater than single-deep storage (typically double-deep storage).

- **Drive-in and drive-through racks** are most often used when there is a need to store a large number of pallet loads of the same SKU and there is a limited amount of floor space available for storage equipment. These two types of racks make effective use of floor space and are able to store pallet loads 5-10 pallets deep.

- **Push-back rack.** A type of storage rack that functions in a manner similar to the drive-in rack is a push-back rack. Pallets (unit loads) are loaded on carts or trays within the confines of the rack. These carts are at a slight incline from front to back and the materials are pushed up the incline against the other pallets already in the rack.

- **Cantilever rack.** A very different type of storage rack is a cantilever rack. This type of storage rack is seen in home centers and facilities that handle and store materials such as lumber, steel sheets and rods and other relatively long or unusually large items.

- **Mobile sliding racks** consist of rows of storage racks that are affixed to a set of rails embedded in the floor. By moving the mobile rows of racks, workers can use one aisle to access several rows of racks.

Repack: Shelving, Bin and Drawer Storage

The storage and handling of small items, such as electronic parts, nuts, bolts, and small assemblies, is a frequent task assigned to material handling workers. These workers may be required to replenish the order-picking area so that items can be picked for shipment or made available for use in putting together kits (kitting).

An example of small parts storage and picking is assembling the nuts and bolts for a homeowner product. Anyone who has attempted to assemble a child's swing set or toy will recall the seemingly huge bag of nuts, bolts, screws and washers that arrives with the item.

Someone at the manufacturer had to pick all these small items from storage and place them in a bag for shipment to the customer. The responsibility of material handling workers is to gather these items in larger quantities and place them in a central working area so that persons placing them in bags can easily access them.

CHAPTER 2

Small bins placed in shelving or racks at a workstation are generally the way to do this. These bin systems are continually replenished by workers.

Shelving
Shelving used for storage is commercial grade. It is usually made from higher gauge metal than household type shelving.

- Shelving is a convenient and cost-effective form of storage.

- Shelving is easily assembled and placed where needed in the facility.

Terms to Know

Push-back rack
A high-density storage system that can hold several units deep on slightly inclined rails. As a unit is removed from the front, the incline causes units behind it to move forward into the front location.

Single-deep storage
Rack that holds only one unit (typically a pallet load) deep.

Vertical lift module (VLM)
Automated storage and retrieval system that moves units or items between levels in a facility.

- Ease of movement and assembly make shelving a logical choice for storage of materials that do not need the bulk of structural steel storage racks to house them.

Supportability. The shelves and vertical supports can be joined by nuts and bolts, clips or by riveting. Facilities must consider the gauge thickness of the metal when choosing shelving. The shelving supports must be able to handle the weight and size of the load.

Drawer storage. Some items stored in a facility may be extremely fragile or valuable. These items must be handled and stored in a safe and secure manner. Storing these materials or items in drawers is a logical way to organize them and to provide needed security and care for them. Storage drawer systems usually involve a storage cabinet.

- A storage cabinet contains multiple drawers that can be locked for security.

- Storage cabinet drawers can be "lined" with protective fabric or rubber matting to protect the contents against scratching or scoring.

Palletized Storage
Pallet materials. Pallets have historically been made of wood. Pallets made from other materials such as plastic, paper, rubber and metal are also used in the modern supply chain. However, regardless of construction material used, the basic design of a pallet is the same. The types of materials used to construct pallets are:

- Corrugated paper - used in some cases to form a light weight pallet.

- Rubber and plastic - used where sanitizing and wash-down capabilities are needed.

- Metal - used to handle extremely heavy loads that other types of pallet materials cannot.

Choice of pallet material. The decision on what type of material to use in the construction of pallets is made by the users of the pallet. There are several considerations involved in deciding which materials are best for a particular use:

- Durability - including the number of trips that the pallet makes into and out of the facility.

- Weight carrying capacity.

- Special applications such as food service or corrosive environments that require a pallet that can be easily cleaned or sanitized.

Key issues in palletizing. A few more points need to be made about pallets in the supply chain.

Materials may arrive for storage on a pallet and even be stored temporarily as a pallet load. Based on demand, some of the items on a pallet may eventually be shipped as cases or as a single item. As a result, a certain number of loads on pallets may be broken apart to provide access to the individual cases.

Not all pallet loads necessarily contain a large quantity of a single material. Pallets generally arrive at a facility as full pallets, but sometimes depart the facility containing many different items called a mixed pallet load. Because pallets are usually more efficient to be handled than individual cases, shipments departing a facility for a specific destination often consist of smaller quantities of many different items. These items are sometimes combined on a single pallet.

Some companies practice pallet pooling in which a large group of companies purchase a pool of pallets that any company in the group may rent. When shipping and receiving, these pallets must be tracked and accounted for just like any other material. This system makes pallets less of a burden on businesses and is more environmentally responsible.

Specialty Containers

Plastic Totes
Plastic totes provide protection and unitizing for materials that enter and leave the facility.

CHAPTER 2

They are available in a wide variety of sizes and shapes; and special designs are also readily available from the makers of these containers. These containers can house almost any kind of material, including bulk materials and liquids. Small plastic totes can be carried by an individual worker to transport small items or orders from one location to another. This is a common use of this type of container.

Metal Containers

Metal containers are a typical protective and unit load formation device used in manufacturing and logistics facilities. Metal is strong, durable and affords a high degree of protection against abuse.

Like plastic totes, metal containers are available in a wide variety of shapes, sizes and features. Metal containers that have solid side-walls made from corrugated steel are very common.

Wire Mesh Containers

Another useful form of metal container is a welded wire mesh container. It has many features of the plastic tote. It can be made to fold or collapse unto itself for ease and efficiency of storage when not in use.

Crates

A crate is a common term for containers made of wood. A wooden crate can be built around almost any item in need of protection. It can be a solid wooden wall enclosure or a shell that provides enough structure to enable the object to be grasped and moved while providing a degree of protection at the same time. Wood is a cheaper material for pallet and container construction. The cost of leaving a wooden device after a single, one-way delivery is smaller in comparison to the alternatives.

Crates for Military Use

The military ships and stores some rather uncommon materials and objects. These materials or objects may not be capable of being housed in conventional containers. The military relies heavily on wooden crates as a means of protecting materials for military use.

The military sometimes ships combustible and/or explosive items. Use of metal containers could cause a problem, especially when shipping ammunition, by emitting sparks from metal shipping or storage enclosures.

Corrugated Paper Pallets and Containers

Great strides have been made in paper technology in recent years. The use of paper and corrugated paper has emerged as a viable form of material for protective packaging.

An increasing number of storage and unit load devices are being made from paper. The corrugated or cardboard box has long been a container of choice for many storage and transportation purposes. It is not unusual to see pallets and pallet boxes made from corrugated paper. The protection level and unit load formation capabilities that these enclosures provide has been improved by applying special coatings to the paper or by blending in chemical additives as the paper is being made. These actions make the containers more resistant to the elements.

Insulation for package contents is provided with the addition of interior packaging materials. Extremes of cold are not often a problem, but heat can present a problem for paper containers for obvious reasons. Chemical additives and coatings can make these containers less susceptible to heat and resistant to fire.

Slip Sheets

Slip sheets are used to ship materials without the bulk and weight of pallets. They are usually made of corrugated material and fit between stacks of containers. They may require transfer to a standard pallet on receipt of the materials using a specially equipped lift truck.

Drums and Barrels

Bulk materials such as powdered goods and liquids are often contained in drums and barrels and can be especially unique in their application in a facility.

Drums and barrels:

• Are usually used to transport and store liquids and powdered or granulated goods in bulk

• Can be metal, plastic or wooden

• Require lift trucks to use special attachments

Other Methods of Storage and Retrieval

Carousels

A carousel is a type of powered storage device that moves either horizontally or vertically. Storage bins are brought to workers who may be either placing items into or retrieving them from storage. Horizontal carousels move on a horizontal plane. The items are stored in baskets or shelves on the carousel.

A vertical carousel moves shelves and bins of materials in an upward and downward circular motion. Vertical carousels resemble a dumb waiter. This unit is usually self-contained.

Did You Know?

The power of pallet pooling

In this age of sustainability, the concept of using/sharing/reusing pallets is notable. Called pallet pooling, this circular loop manages pallets and makes them available for use across many companies and industries.

Some of the benefits of pallet pooling are that companies can:

• Reduce operational costs - no capital outlay for one-way pallets or shipping platforms.

• Gain greater budget flexibility: pay for what is needed, when it's needed

• Solve materials handling requirements with access to advice from industry experts.

• Meet supply needs during times of seasonal or unexpected spikes as equipment is available on-demand.

• Reduce staff costs with no pallet procurement or disposal programs to manage.

• Reduce environmental impact with reusable packaging.

• Save on storage costs by holding less pallet inventory - companies can collect and return pallets to CHEP at any time.

All of the motions take place in an enclosure. The desired materials are brought to an opening in the cabinets for storage and retrieval. An enclosed vertical carousel is often the equipment of choice if security and ease of access are equally important.

CHAPTER 2

Vertical Lift Modules (VLMs)

These are a type of storage equipment that uses both vertical and horizontal areas of a facility in an efficient manner. VLMs resemble a dumb waiter that was seen in many multi-story homes of the past. The principle of moving things from one floor of a home to the other underlies the concept of the VLMs.

VLMs are very similar to carousels in their abilities but VLMs are capable of a higher volume of throughput than both vertical and horizontal carousels. VLMs are used when access to stored materials is needed at different levels or floors. These pieces of storage equipment can be designed so that the openings are accessible to workers at different levels of the facility.

A-Frame Dispensing System

An A-frame dispensing system handles individual items that material handlers pick from unit loads. As the name implies, workers literally open cases or cartons of materials and dispense items out. These items are placed in the appropriate slots in the walls of the device.

A control system tells the slots to release the item onto the belt, picking the desired items to fulfill an order. This process is very similar to the candy dispensing machines seen in break rooms and the halls of hotels and motels but is more highly automated in its operation.

Flow Rack

A flow rack moves boxes, totes or pallets on gravity rollers or skate wheels from the rear to the front of the rack. Materials are loaded at the back end and retrieved at the front. As materials are removed from the lower end, the remaining materials roll forward. These types of racks offer a higher density of storage, require fewer access aisles and use less floor space than traditional pallet racks.

Mezzanine

A mezzanine is a structure built over the top of the other activities in a facility that creates another floor for facility workers to use. It makes use of the unoccupied space that exists over all the other activities going on below. The mezzanine is a relatively inexpensive way to provide additional space for storage, offices or high-security areas.

Shipping and receiving dock areas are often designed with mezzanines because the area above docks is not typically used for high volume storage.

Where travel is permitted under the mezzanine, shelving and bin storage can be built below the mezzanine, creating more space for needed storage.

Automated Storage and Retrieval Systems (AS/RS)

AS/RS are storage and retrieval systems that are different from carousels and VLMs. They tend to be large and use extensive banks of racks to store items. Storage/retrieval machines such as cranes in the center aisle of the AS/RS or shuttles in various storage lanes move items into and out of these systems. AS/RS are designed to store both large and small items such as pallet loads or smaller unit loads of materials.

All AS/RS are automated to varying degrees. Some are so automated that they can store and retrieve materials without direct human involvement. Commands are given to them through computer programs.

Man-on-board AS/RS

The most basic AS/RS used to store and retrieve materials is the man-on-board. This system has an operator who rides along with an order-picker and its load. The man-on-board AS/RS is used for in-aisle picking. The machine can be manually or automatically controlled, but there is an operator present on the machine itself.

Fully Automated Storage and Retrieval Systems

These systems consist of an integrated computer-controlled system that combines:

- The storage medium (rack or shelving)

- Transport mechanism (the crane or shuttle)

- Controls with various levels of automation for fast, accurate and random storage and retrieval of products and materials

The storage/retrieval machine of an AS/RS operates in a narrow aisle in the center of the system, and serves rack openings on both sides of the aisle. It can travel horizontally (along the aisle) and vertically (up and down a rack) at the same time. Because the aisles in this type of operation are very narrow,

the equipment is usually either wire-guided or guided by rails that are built into the floor. There are advantages to this sophisticated system: fewer material handlers are needed; better material control (including security); more efficient use of storage space, and higher throughputs of materials or items.

Warehouse Management System

WMS software is used because there are many questions to be answered when determining storage locations:

- Does the material need to be co-located with other materials that are usually ordered together?

- Does the material need to be stored in a unified form, such as a pallet, which can later be broken down and stored in smaller quantities?

- Does the material have environmental considerations such as protection from extreme temperatures or moisture?

- Does the material require biohazard or other safety considerations?

- Does the material need special packaging?

- Does the material need rack or bulk storage?

- Does the material have a shelf life?

Notes

CHAPTER 3

Order Processing

Overview of Chapter

The purpose of this chapter is to explain how the order process works from the time an order is received from a customer until the time the order is assembled for packaging. Order picking is a critical component of material handling and is starting position for many frontline logistics workers. This chapter will describe the role of frontline workers in ensuring that the order picking process is efficient and accurate.

Objectives

When you have completed this chapter, you will be able to do these things:

1. Describe best practices in order cycle and procurement processes, including information flows.

2. Explain pick ticket inspection.

3. Identify processes for accurately pulling products from storage identified on pick tickets.

4. Explain how audits are conducted to ensure that pulled products are as ordered.

5. Describe staging of pulled products for shipping.

6. Describe steps involved in developing a packing manifest.

Order Cycle Practices

Order Processing

Order processing begins when the seller receives an order and ends when a location (such as a warehouse or distribution center) is authorized to fill the order. Nothing happens until an order is received. The quicker the supplier can receive the order from the customer, the quicker the process can begin.

Once an order is received, it must be screened. First, the supplier decides if it is willing to fill the order based on past payment history provided by the sales department. Then, the supplier determines if it can fill the order; how long it will take to fill it; and whether the customer is willing to wait, if necessary.

Facilities throughout the supply chain have computerized much of the order process. Without an automated decision-making system, the process can take much longer to be filled as the order is shuffled among the sales, customer service, logistics and accounting departments. The paper trail may be haphazard and error prone. As a result, most companies use automated order processing systems.

The order initiates the process of assembling products from various stock locations for a specific customer order. Think of the order in terms of a stock keeping unit or SKU (pronounced skew). A SKU is a number or string of alphabetic and numeric characters that uniquely identifies an item or product. These SKUs could be a universal number, a supplier part number or a unique identifier used by the company.

CHAPTER 3

Terms to Know

Batch Pick
A method of picking orders in which order requirements are aggregated by product location in the warehouse and across orders to reduce movement to and from product locations. The aggregated quantities of each product are then transported to a common area where the individual orders are constructed.

Item
Any unique manufactured or purchased part, material, intermediate, subassembly, or product.

Line
A specific physical space for the manufacture of a product that in a flow shop layout is represented by a straight line.

Order
A general term that may refer to such diverse items as a purchase order, shop order, customer order, planned order, or schedule.

Order Processing
The activity required to administratively process a customer's order and make it ready for shipment or production.

Most companies use their own SKU numbers to label products so they can track their inventory using their own custom database systems.

Order Picking

Importance

A survey of warehousing professionals identified order picking as the highest priority activity for productivity improvements.

First, order picking is the most costly activity in a typical warehouse. Some estimate that more than 60% of all warehouse operating costs can be attributed to order picking related activities. Picking can account for as much as half of the labor costs in a distribution operation, and pickers often spend 50% or more of their time moving from one location to the next.

Second, order picking activities have become more complicated to manage with the introduction of new operating programs such as just-in-time (JIT), cycle reduction as well as new marketing strategies. Many of these programs typically require that smaller orders be delivered to customers more frequently and accurately and that more SKUs be put into the order picking system.

Third, renewed emphasis on quality improvements and customer service have forced managers to re-examine order picking to minimize product damage, reduce transaction times and further improve picking accuracy.

Process

When it is time to ship an order, the warehouse management system (WMS) generates a pick list that indicates the quantities of each item in the order. The order picker instruction process describes the SKU, directs the picker to the SKU pick position, indicates the quantity required and states the customer's name or order identification number.

Order picker instructions must be simple and clear. They must tell the order picker precisely what needs to be done. The instructions can be printed on a paper document, a label, a lighted display with letters and numbers or even through an audio headset. These instructions often include alpha/numeric characters that identify specific aisles or SKU pick positions in the facility.

Keep in mind that a WMS is what allows a pick list to be generated in a productive sequence for the pickers. This means that once an item is received, its location is tracked so it can be retrieved when needed at a later time to fill a customer order. Generating pick lists is a classic example of how the flow of computer-based information is controlled to confirm that everything has a place and a pre-determined use.

An order picker takes the pick list (electronically displayed on a mobile device or on paper) with instructions and retrieves the items in the order in which they appear on the list. This set of steps is designed to take the picker on the shortest path to the items.

This approach can lead to a range of savings including the time it takes the picker to retrieve the order as well as savings in the distance traveled by the picker. In addition, costs can be reduced when multiple orders are picked by a single order picker.

Three common picking schemes are used to organize the picking process:

Area System/Single Order Pick. In this scheme, the picker goes through the warehouse and picks the items on the order—just as a shopper gets items on a grocery list in a supermarket. When the picker takes the items to the shipping area, the work is finished. This system is generally used in small warehouses where there is a set place for each item.

Zone Pick. In this system, the warehouse is divided into zones and order pickers only work in their own zone or area.

First, the order is divided into defined zones. Then each picker selects items for their zone and sends the items to a general area for final assembly before shipment. Each order must be

handled separately before another is begun by the picker.

Zones are usually set up for related parts. For example, parts that need to be stored in a freezer or that are often ordered together could be in one zone.

Multi-order Batch Pick. With this scheme, pickers handle multiple orders at a time within a defined zone. Pickers collect all the items they need for that group of orders. Then, the items are sent to the general collection area where they are sorted into individual orders for shipment.

Within those three schemes, picking can be carried out in three ways:

Single-order picking. One picker in one zone of the picking area collects the items for a single order.

Batch picking. A picker assembles all the items for a group of orders at one time.

Pick-by-line or Pick-to-zero. For this approach, the exact numbers of cases or items within one product line are present for picking. The picker then picks the required number of cases or items from one product line (pick-by-line) to fill waiting customer orders.

CHAPTER 3

The picking may continue until that line is exhausted (pick-to-zero).

Processes for Improving Accuracy and Efficiency

There are ways to improve order-picking accuracy and productivity to meet increased order demand. Some may be implemented without increasing staff or making significant investments in automated equipment. Others may involve increased use of various technologies.

Three examples of improved processes without the addition of technology are:

Pick task simplification. It is not uncommon for unnecessary steps to creep into picking processes over time. By re-evaluating the process and eliminating and/or combining order picking tasks, the pick process can be simplified, saving time and effort by pickers. Even when work elements cannot be eliminated, it is sometimes possible to combine certain tasks and even orders to improve order processing productivity.

Order batching. Grouping two or more orders in a single batch reduces travel time by order

pickers. For example, if an order picker picks one order with two items while traveling 100 feet, the distance traveled per pick is 50 feet. However, if the picker simultaneously picks two orders with four items, the distance traveled per pick is cut to 25 feet.

Moving inventory to a forward pick location. This process, often used in larger warehouses, condenses the pick path by grouping needed inventory in a forward, consolidated location. For instance, the orders for a single day can be batched together so that all products are combined and brought to a consolidated, forward pick location. This site is often located by the outbound staging area, significantly cutting the distance and time that an order picker spends traveling and/or searching for needed inventory. It is one of the most effective ways to improve picking productivity and accuracy.

Some examples of improving processes with technology:

Bar codes. These are widely used to identify individual storage and picking locations as well as individual products down to the SKU level. Scanning relevant bar codes during the picking process records and confirms picking accuracy electronically.

Radio frequency data communication terminals. These mobile devices provide real-time communication between designated workstations and the WMS. The terminals may be mounted on trucks as well as pickers. They typically include a bar code scanner to ensure scanning all items during the pick process. Scanners can be built into the mobile device or fitted as a ring on a finger to enable pickers to use both hands for picking not scanning, improving efficiency.

Pick-to-light systems. This technology combines various forms of racking that holds inventory, LED lights at each pick location and bar codes. Pick-to-light systems both direct order pickers' paths and immediately informs them of the accuracy of their pick while keeping their hands free for picking activities.

By scanning the bar code on an electronic or paper pick list, the pick-to-light system illuminates a light at the next pick location. When the picker selects the item, the bar code on it is scanned. A red or green light is then illuminated, indicating a correct (green) or incorrect (red) pick. This gives the picker immediate feedback on the pick's accuracy, allowing the person to either move on to the next pick or correct the error.

Put-to-light systems. These are essentially the reverse of pick-to-light systems. Instead of identifying locations to pick items, put-to-light identifies a location for the worker to place an item to fill an order. These systems also use bar codes, scanners and lights to both direct the worker's path and accuracy of the put task.

Voice technology. Wearing a headset, the picker hears voice instructions directing picking activities from location to number of items to pick. The picker then selects the required items and speaks through a microphone to confirm the pick. Often, an address number at each location must be repeated by the picker to make sure the correct items were picked. As with pick-to-light, the picker's hands are free.

Order Inspection and Accuracy

Once picked and assembled, orders must be inspected for accuracy. The order picker must verify that the quantity picked is the quantity required or note any differences. This will eliminate confusion in shipping and at the customer's receiving operation. This must also be done to ensure the picker's accountability.

Terms to Know

Order processing departments typically use the following terminology:

Item
A specific SKU.

Line
Multiple requirements for a particular SKU, i.e., the number of items of a particular SKU.

Order
Customer requirements as specified by a picking document.

Order Pickers
The people who select, count and deliver customer merchandise (orders) to shipping.

If an item is out of stock, the information will be sent to the order department to fix the original documents. A packing list is enclosed for each outgoing order, showing what items were picked. The customer can then check the packing list to make sure all items are present.

CHAPTER 3

There are two ways to verify that the picked merchandise and the picked quantity are correct— either manually (visual) or by bar code scanning.

Manually. This approach requires a packing employee to visually compare the picked merchandise and the packing slip items. If there is a match, the employee prepares the package for shipment. If there is not a match, and there is a shortage of the picked merchandise, the packing employee places the picked merchandise and packing slip together on a problem order shelf. If there is no match because of an excess of picked merchandise, then the packing employee prepares the package for shipment and places surplus merchandise on a problem order shelf.

Disadvantages of the manual method are possible verification errors and lack of online tracking of the order. Advantages are large-volume handling, easy employee training and the ability to handle a large number of customers.

Hand-Held barcode scanning. In this customer order check method, the packing employee uses a hand-held device to scan the barcode of each piece of picked merchandise. The packer scans the customer's barcode label on

the packing slip; scans the barcode of each piece of picked merchandise; and packs the merchandise into the shipping container. The scanning device establishes a record that the customer's merchandise was handled at the marshalling area. The barcode scanning merchandise verification method is most widely used in the retail store distribution industry.

Disadvantages are that it requires increased investment, greater employee training and a barcode label. Advantages are a high degree of accuracy, high-volume handling and the ability to handle a wide variety of SKUs.

Staging of Pulled Products for Shipping

Preparations for dispatch

After picking, goods are brought together and consolidated to complete orders for delivery to customers. This can involve packing into outer cases and cartons and stretch- and shrink-wrapping for load protection and stability.

It may also involve final postponement activities and value added services, such as kitting and labeling.

packaged and supplied together as one unit. For example, when ordering a computer online, a customer may select memory, drives, peripherals and software from several alternatives. The supplier then creates a customized kit that is assembled and shipped as one unit.

Marshalling and Staging

Goods are marshalled or gathered together to form loads in the dispatch area. Then, they are loaded onto vehicles to send to the next point in the supply chain. This may be directly to the customer or to a distribution center, port or airport for the next transport leg.

Loads on over-the-road trucks might be floor loaded, which makes better use of the trailer cube but takes longer because boxes or cases must be handled individually. Loads can also be palletized and segregated by product or groups of products. These methods can make the receiving process easier and shorten the carrier's time spent loading and unloading.

The inbound-outbound staging activity is one of the critical activities in shipping and receiving. Enough space must be available as close as possible to the dock doors to accommodate the inbound and outbound capacity for a full delivery truck. This allows for increased inventory accuracy, reduced product damage and greater employee productivity.

Other storage space needs at the dock include sufficient space for empty shipping and receiving devices (pallets, carts, return-to-vendor containers and trash containers). The best dock area allows mobile equipment to travel between the dock plate and the staging area and between the staging and storage areas. The staging area requires vehicular

Terms to Know

Staging
The process of pulling material for an order from inventory before the material is required and collecting it all in a single location, staging. This action is often taken to identify shortages, but it can lead to increased problems in availability and inventory accuracy.

Stock Keeping Unit
A single inventory item is an SKU. For example, a shirt in six colors and five sizes would represent 30 different SKUs.

Zone Pick
A method of subdividing a pick list by areas within a warehouse for more efficient and rapid order picking. A zone-picked order must be grouped to a single location before delivery or must be delivered to different locations, such as work centers.

traffic aisles that connect the dock to the storage area.

The next activity in the preparation for shipping is creating a packing manifest that ensures the customer's order was handled and processed by the distribution facility. This activity can be a manual operation or a bar code scanning operation as noted earlier.

This may be the final activity in the order picking process, or this activity may be performed during the packaging process as explained in the next chapter.

Notes

CHAPTER 4

Packaging and Shipment

Overview of Chapter

The purpose of this chapter is to explain how orders are packaged and prepared for shipping. One of the primary concerns of packaging and shipping is ensuring that the product arrives at its destination undamaged. This chapter will describe types of packaging materials, shipping accuracy and basic principles of loading containers.

Objectives

When you have completed this chapter, you will be able to do these things:

1. Identify the process for selecting appropriate packing materials to package products.

2. Describe selection of packaging tools best suited for handling and packaging products.

3. Explain typical steps to protect products from weather.

4. Describe the process to ensure that outbound product counts are accurate and products are free from defects.

5. Describe the process for verifying outbound products against customer orders.

6. Describe correct product labeling in accordance with domestic and international regulations and common company policies.

7. Identify steps to verify that the right packages are securely loaded into the right trailer.

8. Identify steps to ensure that packages are securely loaded into trailers and correctly distributed based on safe loading procedures.

Packaging

There can be up to three levels of packaging depending on the item being shipped:

• The primary package is the box, can, blister pack or another container that holds the actual product.

• The secondary package is usually a carton that groups a number of primary packages for easier handling.

• The third layer, the transport package, is usually a pallet with a protective covering such as a polyurethane sheet.

This chapter will focus on secondary and transport packaging and factors involved in choosing the best packaging materials.

Definition

Packaging is the process of using materials to contain and protect a product during handling,

CHAPTER 4

storage and shipping. The main function of packaging is to contain a product so that it can be safely transferred to its point of destination. Preparing a product for shipment is a critical step in the supply chain.

Basics

How a product is packaged has a direct impact on how it is stored, where it is stored and how it is moved through a warehouse. Most packaging is done in a repack area or a small packaging line within the warehouse. This is in contrast to full-case or bulk-picking areas.

Repack or small package lines are very common in warehouses that handle general merchandise, health and beauty products and pharmaceuticals. There are warehouses and distribution centers that handle only full case or bulk merchandise. In these instances, packaging is limited to palletizing or combining full cases in some manner. Most repack operations use conveyors to collect the products into master cartons or totes. Pickers put up to 50 items in a master carton, seal it and send it on to the shipping department.

Packaging for Protection

As items move through the supply chain especially during transport, they must be protected against a wide range of possible threats including:

• Shock

• Compression

• Vibration

• Moisture

• Heat

• Cold

The level of protection needed often depends not only on the type of product being shipped but also on the value of the items. Different packing materials can be used to provide additional protection when necessary. These materials include: corrugated dividers, moisture barriers, cardboard inserts, paper filler material, foam-filled cushions and foam peanuts. These materials can be inserted into the outer package to fill voids and protect the inner package.

In many cases, dunnage material is placed between cases or pallets for additional product protection. The specific packaging needs depend on the product and how susceptible it is to damage. There are a number of factors to be considered when choosing the type and extent of packaging:

Three primary levels of packaging:

1. Primary package

2. Secondary package

3. Transport package

- Fragility of the product

- Storage and transport conditions such as heat and moisture

- Possible interactions between the product and the packaging material

- Number of units that will be shipped together

- Type of transport

- Loading and unloading methods to be used

- Customer shipping instructions

- Cost requirements

- Environmental impacts of disposal

Carrier Requirements

A carrier's tariffs and classifications can influence the type of packaging and packing methods that are used. Carriers established these classifications for two main reasons.

First, carriers want shippers to make every effort to put as much on a trailer as they can within the limits of weight and cube (volume). The loading of the trailer (in terms of how items are stacked and how the load is packed from front to back) has more to do with damage than the individual packaging.

However, in the package design process, companies do take into account how the product will be packaged and what affect it may have on the cost of shipping. IKEA, the Swedish-based home furnishings chain, designs many of its products so they can be shipped in a dense form. Such products are often purchased unassembled in retail stores, and customers can easily take them home in their cars.

Terms to Know

Impact of Packaging on Operations

- Product protection
- Line-side pack quantity
- Trailer cube/weight utilization
- Warehouse space utilization
- Material handling efficiency
- Product identity (visual control)
- Ergonomics
- Environmental concerns
- Total costs

Second, carrier specifications for protective packaging cut the likelihood of damage to products being carried. This, in turn, reduces the amount of loss and damage claims placed against the carrier.

Unit Loads

Once goods have been packaged for processing and movement throughout a facility, the goods must be prepared for shipment. The items are most commonly collected into unit loads for easier transport. There are several types of unit loads.

CHAPTER 4

- Wooden pallets are the most common unit load used in distribution operations. They are made to standard sizes for use of standard storage and handling equipment such as forklifts and stacker trucks.

- Master cartons or plastic totes are quite commonly used for small repack type items.

- There are also specialty containers that are basically box pallets made of wire, plastic or metal. These are primarily used for liquids when the possibility of puncture is a concern.

Palletized Loads

There are different ways to secure palletized goods for transport.

Pallet wrappers. These use a stretch film pallet wrapper or stretch wrapper. Plastic film protects the materials and keeps them together on a pallet. The film is water resistant and is stretched tightly over and around the pallet and its contents to form an almost water-tight enclosure.

By applying the film in a tight pattern, the pallet wrapper ensures the load is contained and stabilized. The load is secured to the pallet as the wrap spirals upward and downward around and over the load.

Powered stretch wrappers. Powered wrappers are usually used when large numbers of pallets need to be wrapped. The loaded pallet is placed on a turntable, and the film is attached. Then the turntable is activated and the roll of film moves up and down on a track, ensuring that the pallet load is covered from top to bottom as the pallet turns.

Automatic stretch wrappers. This is a step up from the basic powered stretch wrapper. These wrappers are completely automated and are usually part of a conveyor system.

Strapping. Straps can be made of plastic or metal. Like wraps, straps can be applied manually or by machine.

When Packaging Becomes Waste

Another important consideration when choosing packaging materials is the waste that will be produced. Most packaging discussed in this section will be used only once and then discarded as waste. This has an environmental

impact and increases costs. As a result, many industries have begun using packaging that can be recycled or reused.

Labeling

Items must be labeled properly to ensure safe and accurate transport through the supply chain. In addition to providing basic product information, labels are subjected to various rules and regulations. There are both general product labeling standards and federal and international requirements for shipping labels. As with packaging, there are different levels of labeling from the retail label to the shipping carton labels. For our purposes, we will focus on shipping labels.

Basic Label Information

Shipping labels typically include a wide variety of information. Technology provides the ability to include relatively large amounts of data on a small label such as a bar code or RFID tag. Many packages include both long-hand information labels as well as bar codes. For example, some printed labels include a bar code that contains all of the shipping information, but the printed label still includes the printed information of the addressee and addressor in human readable form.

Accuracy & Quality Control

Verifying Customer Orders

An order must be checked for accuracy before it is shipped. Accuracy involves several criteria. It means that the proper product, in the proper amount and in the proper condition is selected and verified against a customer order. Once a verified order has been assembled, workers must ensure that the correct items end up on the proper trailer for shipment.

Checks can be performed manually, in which a worker visually inspects the items for defects,

counts them and verifies them against a customer order form. In larger operations, checks are performed via a semi- or fully-automated system, where items are scanned, counted and verified by a machine using bar codes, measurements and other standardized information.

Packages must be checked against customer orders to ensure the following criteria are met:

• The proper product(s)

• In the proper quantity are

• Free from visual or obvious defect

Verifying Correct Shipments

Usually, the checking function is done in the loading or staging area of the shipping department because it is the last step before an order leaves a facility. This is also a checking point because it is the place where the entire order finally comes together from the various parts of the warehouse. This is especially true of large warehouses where the order may come from six or seven different areas. At this point in the supply chain, it is critical that the proper orders end up on the proper trailers headed to the proper locations.

CHAPTER 4

An important document at this stage is the shipping manifest. It lists all of the items in a shipment whether the load is to be delivered to a single destination or to multiple destinations. Manifests usually list the items, piece count, total weight and the destination name and address for each destination in a load. Loads should be checked against the manifest before being placed on the trailer. In larger operations, this is done automatically via bar code scanning.

Loading & Shipment

Loading Safety

There are certain activities required to ensure that trailers are loaded safely:

- Loading equipment is only used by certified operators

- Trucks or trailers are securely chocked prior to entry by a forklift

- Hydraulic dock levelers are properly positioned for safe entry

- Pallets are checked to ensure they have not shifted or separated

- Heavy pallets are placed in the front of the trailer to avoid sudden shifts in weight if the driver must stop quickly

- Proper lifting techniques are used by workers when loading items manually

Next, the unit-load pallets are stowed into a waiting truck trailer, railcar or container van. Many companies use special software to plan and configure loads.

The software recognizes various constraints, such as cartons that cannot be laid on their sides or have other cartons placed on top of them. It also takes into account the load's center of gravity and the allowable weights on axles. This planning function is usually handled by the transportation department.

Loading Process

The loading process is important because it is the final time the distribution center can impact the condition and accuracy of the order. At this point, all pieces of the order should be complete and assembled in the staging area for loading.

In facilities that use sorters, cases are loaded continuously throughout the day into an awaiting trailer. Trailers are assigned to a specific door to receive a specific order.

The cases or totes come down a conveyor, directly into the trailer.

It is at as this point that many facilities conduct a final accuracy check. This function can be performed by the Inventory Control or Loss Prevention department. This is also the time and place where specific service failure problems can be addressed. For example, if there is a problem that requires detailed checking of an order, Loss Prevention may check every case and every pallet that is loaded for a specific order. They may even photograph the order as it is loaded.

Loading Techniques

Learning to correctly load a trailer requires skill and experience. There are many factors that determine how the load is arranged.

Trailers can be loaded with a single-stop load, which means the entire load is being delivered to one facility with no other stops in between. Trailers can also be loaded with multiple-stop loads which mean that several orders to different facilities are loaded onto one trailer. This usually requires that the orders be separated to facilitate unloading at each facility. Separating the loads can be done in several ways such as load bars with slip sheets, netting, load walls and strapping.

Floor Loading

Floor loading is when boxes or totes are placed directly on the floor of the trailer and stacked, often to the ceiling. Floor loading is labor intensive because each box must be handled individually. It is also critical to ensure that heavy items are not placed on top of light items and to adhere to directions such as "This Side Up" and "Fragile".

Loading Palletized Goods

More and more, customers require that their orders be palletized and stretch wrapped because it saves time in loading and unloading. For example, a floor loaded trailer may take up to five hours to unload, but a palletized load can be unloaded in as little as 20 to 30 minutes.

Securing the Load

Once the trailer is checked and loaded, the load must be secured so it will arrive in good condition. This can be a challenging task. There are several methods used for securing loads in a trailer such as: load bars, straps, rope, airbags and cargo walls. When determining how to secure a load, companies must consider cost

and ability to have the equipment returned after delivery. Some systems require specially equipped trailers. For example, straps require that the trailer have interior rails to secure the straps.

While palletizing loads is more productive for the receiving operation, it is more costly for the shipper, and it reduces the cube utilization of the trailer.

Stretch wrapping helps this problem by allowing loaders to stack goods higher on pallets, taking more advantage of the available cube. For example, stretch wrapping a pallet allows the loader to stack goods up to 7-feet high on a pallet.

Slight clearances must be maintained between pallets to allow for loading and unloading. Bracing or inflatable dunnage bags are used to fill narrow empty spaces. When inflated, they fill the empty space and function as both a cushion and a brace.

Even when cargoes are properly braced, various forces such as vibration, pitch and roll can cause damage. For example, continued vibrations may loosen screws on machinery or

CHAPTER 4

Some goods are so heavy that they use up a container's weight capacity without filling its cubic capacity (a situation called weighing out). These loads, such as heavy machinery, must be carefully braced, and the weight must be distributed as evenly as possible. In highway trailers, for example, it is dangerous to have one side loaded more heavily than the other. In addition, the load should be distributed evenly over the axles.

Third-party Carrier Loading

Third-party freight carriers often have their own requirements that must be followed when packing and loading a shipment. The primary concern of carriers is the efficient use of their equipment. Therefore, the scheduling of outbound loads is critical. The carrier must know how many trailers are needed for the next day's shipment so the trailers can be spotted in the proper door and ready for the next day. Quite often, trailers are spotted at night or on an off-shift so they do not congest the shipping process.

cause the contents of some bags or packages to settle, changing the type of support they give to the materials packed above them.

For products that present this problem, special preloading vibrators are used to cause the load to settle immediately. A typical phrase used in many loading operations is "high and tight", and this is a good rule of thumb when loading trailers.

Trailer spotting is when yards use spotter trucks, also called yard mules, to move trailers around the yard instead of the delivery driver. This allows the driver to drop one load and pick up another without waiting for loading and unloading.

Another concern of carriers is that trailers are loaded correctly to reduce errors and avoid damages. Carrier claims for damages during transport can result in a significant expense to the carrier and supplier. This is especially important when handling multiple-stop loads — each stop must be clearly separated so the driver knows what to deliver to each stop and frequent handling of each order is minimized. For single stop loads, only the end of the trailer needs to be secured to prevent the product from shifting or falling.

Terms to Know

Dunnage
Inexpensive or waste material used to protect cargo from shifting during transport.

Packaging
The process of using materials to contain and protect a product during handling, storage and shipping.

Tariff
A tax on imports or exports.

Notes

CHAPTER 5

CHAPTER 5

Inventory Control

Overview of Chapter

The purpose of this chapter is to explain how inventory is managed and controlled throughout the supply chain with a special emphasis on warehousing. Inventory control is a major part of logistics. To ensure accuracy, companies must know where products are throughout the entire life cycle of the product. This chapter wiiil describe the various methods that companies use to track and store inventory.

Objectives

When you have completed this chapter, you will be able to do these things:

1. Describe fundamentals of inventory control.

2. List the most common inventory control systems.

3. Explain methods for accurate inventory counting.

4. Describe methods for capturing logistics information.

5. Describe reverse logistics.

Inventory Control Fundamentals

Inventories are materials and supplies carried on hand either for sale or for use in the production process. Inventory control is the process of identifying materials, managing storage space and tracking and controlling those materials.

Inventory control is one of the basics of warehousing and distribution. Companies must know what they have on hand and where it is. What makes the process complicated is the unique requirements of various companies. For instance, some companies must have the ability to place an item on hold, or they might have to reserve a specific amount of inventory for a specific customer. These controls will be discussed later in this chapter.

Types of Inventory

There are many types of inventory. The type of inventory determines the treatment it receives throughout the supply chain. For example:

• Raw material stock consists of component inventory used to feed into production or manufacturing lines.

• Work-in-process (WIP) is made up of partially finished goods between steps in the manufacturing process.

• Finished goods consist of inventory that comes to the warehouse or distribution center packaged and ready to ship. Finished goods inventory is the primary focus of this chapter.

Inventory levels are based on statistical analysis of product movement and include the amount of inventory needed to fill orders in the immediate future based on the company's goals for inventory turns. Many suppliers have seasonal inventories that can be significant, (e.g., retail distribution centers that stock Christmas inventories). In some cases, these temporary inventory peaks can be double the normal inventory.

Inventory peaks can be a major headache for distribution managers. They may force managers to go offsite for temporary storage, which creates a whole new level of inventory control issues such as offsite staffing, security and equipment.

Levels of Inventory Management

Inventory is managed at two primary levels. Each item or unit load is handled, stored and recorded, but the entire inventory of a warehouse/distribution center also needs to be controlled.

Aggregate inventory management involves total inventory movement rather than moving individual items. Inventory turn rate is the key component of total inventory management. A simple formula for inventory turn is to divide total dollars shipped annually by the average monthly inventory on hand plus safety stock which varies by company based on product need.

Item inventory management deals with inventory at the item level. At this level, the importance of individual items is assigned. Frontline logistics workers work mostly with item inventory management.

Inventory type 1: Raw Materials

Inventory type 2: Work-in-Process

Inventory type 3: Finished Goods

CHAPTER 5

Think About It!

Inventory Turn

Calculating inventory turnover is something that businesses do to assess competitiveness, project profits and generally figure out how well they are doing in their industry.

Calculating Basic Inventory Turn Rate

Bob's Tackle Shop had an average inventory cost of $6,000 for the fishing lure department last year. He sold $30,000 of fishing lures at cost last year. His turn rate for the year was 5 times ($30,000/$6,000).

This year, Bob liquidated slow moving items from his fishing lure inventory. His inventory cost dropped to $5,000 for the year, but he still sold $30,000 of fishing lures. His turn rate became 6 times, and he freed up $1,000 to use on other expenses.

What Different Rates Mean

A high inventory turn may sound good because it usually indicates that a high volume of product is being sold. However, a high turn rate may be a warning that:

- Inventory levels are too low, which may indicate that selection is limited

- Prices may be too low, resulting in high volume of sales but low profit margins

- There may be too much time being spent receiving, stocking and placing orders

- A low inventory turn may indicate that:

- Pricing may be too high

- Items in the department may not match customer buying habits

- Products may need better marketing

Inventory Control Systems

Warehouse Management System

The most widely used inventory management system in distribution operations is the warehouse management system (WMS). While this software is heavily used by the inventory control department, it is also widely used by frontline workers. Most data entries into this system are done through hand-held devices that capture bar coded inventory information as materials are entering, leaving or moving through a facility.

A WMS allows employees to identify a variety of data such as quantity, location, status and other relevant information. Information is entered into the system when the product is received and is then used to track the item within the facility. Instead of manually entering the information, modern technology has provided the ability to scan items directly into the system using bar codes primarily or RFID tags infrequently.

A WMS also gives workers a real-time view of the location and quantity of inventory available. It provides direction to material handlers, order pickers and shipping and receiving workers.

Inventory Control Methods

Just-in-time Inventory Control

Just-in-time (JIT) inventory control has gained wide acceptance in both manufacturing and logistics. The concept of JIT is to produce precisely the necessary units in the necessary quantities at the necessary time.

Despite these advantages of JIT, there are also a few disadvantages. It may, for example, lead to increased traffic flows due to the need for smaller but more frequent deliveries of goods to the customer.

A WMS allows employees to identify a variety of data such as quantity, location, status and other relevant information.

JIT is not the right approach for every supply chain. It does not work well in job shops, which do not use production lines, and it is not as relevant to process manufacturing as to discrete parts manufacturing.

By its very nature, JIT keeps current inventory levels low, which can be a problem if there is an interruption in the flow of those goods at any point in the supply chain. This shortcoming of JIT became very apparent as the world worked to smooth out supply chain kinks during the Covid pandemic.

The JIT concept, developed by Japanese businesses and closely tied to the Toyota production system, challenges the foundations of classical inventory theory in reference to the production of goods. Some of the concepts underlying JIT are:

• Minimize inventory.

• Produce only the exact number of units needed at the required time.

• Understand that producing one extra piece is just as bad as being one piece short.

• Consider anything over the minimum amount required as waste.

• Respond quickly to changes in demand.

As a result, JIT manufacturers work with their suppliers, warehouses and distributors to switch from large shipments of materials that go to central receiving facilities to small, frequent shipments that go directly from trucks to the factory floor. Most JIT producers also have a similar program on the outbound side, using small frequent deliveries to minimize their inventory of finished goods.

It is important to review the consequences of JIT regarding material handling. JIT has caused the definition of material handling to evolve from a simple definition of "moving material" to providing all the "rights". Some of these rights in the following terms:

• **Right amount.** The JIT inventory management movement focuses attention on the right amount of inventory in both manufacturing and distribution. A positive aspect of JIT is its questioning attitude regarding inventory levels. Instead of automatically thinking of

CHAPTER 5

having inventories, with JIT the idea is to automatically think in terms of reducing inventories or eliminating them altogether.

- **Right material.** The two most common errors made in order picking are picking the wrong material and picking the wrong amount. Picking the right material is not an easy task, especially in facilities that are complex because of the large number of line items and the type of product being handled.

Think About It

ABC Inventory Control Principles

There are no fixed amounts for each class of inventory. Different proportions can be applied based on objective and criteria. "A" items typically account for a large proportion of the overall value but a small percentage of number of items.

Typical breakouts of the A-B-C classification are:

- A items - 20% of the items that account for 70% of the annual consumption value of the items

- B items - 30% of the items that account for 25% of the annual consumption value of the items

- C items - 50% of the items that account for 5% of the annual consumption value of the items

- Item ratio: 20% + 30% + 50% = 100%

- Item value ratio: 70% + 25% + 5% = 100%

Related Term: Pareto Principle, or the 80-20 Rule. ABC Analysis is similar to the Pareto principle which states that 80% of results come from 20% of input. The principle was coined by Joseph Juran, a quality control expert.

- **Right condition.** The third element in the evolving definition of material handling emphasizes the need to provide material in the right condition. To enhance responsiveness in a JIT environment, there is a heightened need to move, store, control and protect materials in the right sequence.

- **Right time and place.** The need for the material handling system to move, store, control and protect material at the right time and place is increasingly important in a world of next-day or even same day delivery, especially with e-commerce items.

Another example of the impact of JIT is the increasing use of rapid, just-in-time JIT replenishment strategies. Just-in-time replenishment is a system of scheduling inbound deliveries to arrive at the receiving dock just in time to replenish the workstation or ready reserve position.

This philosophy has an impact on reducing the required on-hand reserve stock inventory and emphasizes the receiving and shipping dock areas and operations rather than storage-pick areas and operations. Retail store distributors are an example of an industry that has implemented this kind of across-the-dock or quick-response distribution program.

ABC Inventory Control

Normally, A-B-C inventory analysis refers to demand. That is, A items are the fastest movers, B items are next and C items are the slowest. In some cases, high value items may be added to the A item list regardless of movement. It is based on the principle that if you control the fastest moving and/or highest cost items, the slower moving, lower cost items will not have a significant impact.

Generally, A items represent 70% of the value of goods moved. C items represent only 5% of the value of the goods moved but may account for half of the items in quantity. A items are usually stored closest to shipping or receiving areas for easy access.

FIFO vs. LIFO

First-in-First-Out (FIFO) or Last-in-First-Out (LIFO) are two methods of inventory management. They determine when an item is used or picked for delivery based on when the product or material arrived at the facility.

FIFO (First-in-First-Out). This method says that the first item received is the first item to be sold or delivered. This method is by far the most widely used for many reasons. For example, food items need to be shipped in the order that they were received or produced to prevent spoilage. Pharmaceutical items also have a critical shelf life (the length of time that a product remains fit for use). In general, it is a good idea to use FIFO to avoid aging of the product because of dust, damage and infestation.

LIFO (Last-in-First-Out). This method assumes that the last item to be placed in stock is the first item to be sold or delivered. While this method is not widely used, there are some instances when it is necessary. For instance, in the case of retail electronics where models change frequently, companies may want the

Terms To Know

Aggregate Inventory Management

Establishing the overall level (dollar value) of inventory desired and implementing controls to achieve this goal.

Cycle Count

An inventory accuracy audit technique where inventory is counted on a cyclical schedule rather than once a year. A cycle inventory count is usually taken on a regular, defined basis (often more frequently for high-value or fast-moving items and less frequently for low-value or slow-moving items). Most effective cycle counting systems require the counting of a certain number of items every workday with each item counted at a prescribed frequency. The key purpose of cycle counting is to identify items in error, thus, triggering research, identification, and elimination of the cause of errors.

First-in-First-Out (FIFO)

A method of inventory valuation for accounting purposes. The accounting assumption is that the oldest inventory (first in) is the first to be used (first out), but there is no necessary relationship with the actual physical movement of specific items.

Fixed Order Quantity Ordering

An inventory system, such as economic order quantity, in which the same order quantity is used from order to order. The time between orders (order period) then varies from order to order.

CHAPTER 5

newest model shipped to coincide with ads that are running for a sale. This method is not used as much in practice as it is by accounting and financial offices to change the way a company's inventory is valued for tax purposes or how it affects their financial performance.

Terms To Know

Inventory

1) Those stocks or items used to support production (raw materials and work-in-process items), supporting activities (maintenance, repair, and operating supplies), and customer service (finished goods and spare parts).

   Demand for inventory may be dependent or independent. Inventory functions are anticipation, hedge, cycle (lot size), fluctuation (safety, buffer or reserve), transportation (pipeline), and service parts.

2) All the money currently tied up in the system. As used in theory of constraints, inventory refers to the equipment, fixtures, buildings, and so forth that the system owns - as well as inventory in the forms of raw materials, work-in-process, and finished goods.

Inventory Turnover

The number of times that an inventory cycles, or turns over, during the year. A frequently used method to compute inventory turnover is to divide the average inventory level into the annual cost of sales.

For example, an average inventory of $3 million divided into an annual cost of sales of $21 million means that inventory turned over 7 times.

When to Order

Another aspect of inventory control is determining when products need to be restocked. There are three basic approaches.

Cyclical ordering is a time-based system. Items are ordered based on anticipated usage according to a predetermined schedule. Inventory levels must be monitored between ordering times to ensure that the order schedule keeps stock quantities at sufficient levels to fulfill orders.

A fixed-order quantity system is based on order points and quantities instead of time. When inventory levels fall to a certain point, items are re-ordered. Ordering is planned so that inventories do not exceed or fall below certain amounts.

Material requirements planning (MRP) is a computer-based method of inventory management. The computer holds information regarding a master production or delivery schedule. The system monitors stock levels and expected production and determines how much needs to be ordered at any given time.

Inventory Accountability

Inventory management is based upon accurate inventory counts. Companies must know how much of an item is in stock to know what they are able to deliver at any given time. For this reason, inventory management is a critical part of the supply chain.

Different links in the supply chain will manage inventory differently, but the first and most important aspect of inventory control is to know the number of each SKU held in your facility. Taking inventory involves: counting, recording the count, recounting and collecting the count information. There are different count methods based on the size and type of facility or when the counting takes place:

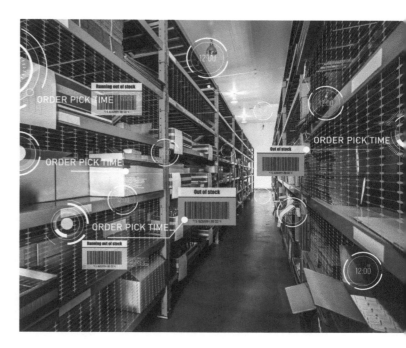

- **Manual count.** In this method, an employee walks the facility with a printed form or hand-held device, manually counts the items and records them or compares them to a booked inventory count (the amount that is supposed to be there).

- **Automated count.** This method utilizes bar codes or RFID tags to scan items as they are received at a facility. An employee uses a hand-held scanner to read the bar code or tag which automatically adds the inventory count into the WMS.

In addition to these count types, there are different count methods that determine when inventory counts are taken and recorded. These include:

- **Random count.** A worker counts a specific SKU. The count is made to verify the exact amount which is recorded in the inventory control system. This can be done either by specific location or as a total of all locations for a specific SKU.

- **Cycle count.** A cycle count occurs when inventory is counted based on A-B-C analysis. While it varies based on company policy, typically, A items are counted 8 times a year, B items 4 times a year and C items twice a year.

Cycle counting has become the popular method for most companies especially in large warehouses and distribution centers where taking a physical inventory involves shutting down the operation for several days. Companies have also found that wall–to-wall physical counts tend to create as many errors as they find in the process. In addition to identifying errors in inventory records, cycle counting helps identify the reasons why inventory errors are occurring.

- **Wall-to-wall physical count.** A physical inventory count is usually conducted to verify inventory amounts for financial purposes. The amount of inventory on-hand at the end of the year is important to businesses for accounting and tax purposes, so special counts are sometimes required for this purpose.

CHAPTER 5

Capturing Logistics Information

Most mistakes in logistics records are caused by human entry error. Automating data entry and retrieval processes is a way to reduce these errors. Most logistic software systems are designed to integrate automatic identification technologies, meaning that information is captured and transmitted into the system at the same time.

Automated Data Capture

Automated systems work by using labels or devices that can be scanned. These devices and systems increase accuracy by eliminating human replication of the information. The ability to communicate accurately, rapidly and economically across the supply chain depends on broad-scale application of automatic identification, especially bar codes. To work with an automated system, workers need to understand the flow of materials and information within the system.

Flow. In automated systems, the flow of materials is controlled so there is little or no mistake as to where they are going and who will move them with what equipment. By electronically obtaining data via labeling, bar coding and data entry into a computer, personnel are told to take a given item to a specific location in the warehouse or distribution center.

Directional devices. As items are moved on automated conveyors, directional devices control the flow and point them in the right direction. These devices may include pushers, pullers, diverters, tilt trays and directional shoes. Each controls the movement of materials in a predetermined direction without human involvement.

Terms To Know

Just-in-Time (JIT)

A philosophy of manufacturing based on planned elimination of all waste and on continuous improvement of productivity. It encompasses the successful execution of all manufacturing activities required to produce a final product, from design engineering to delivery, and includes all stages of conversion from raw material onward.

The primary elements of JIT are to have only the required inventory when needed; to improve quality to zero defects; to reduce lead times by reducing setup times, queue lengths, and lot sizes; to incrementally revise the operations themselves; and to accomplish these activities at minimum cost. In the broad sense, it applies to all forms of manufacturing (job shop, process, and repetitive) and to many service industries as well.

Signage and Labeling

In addition to identifying and labeling individual items and unit loads, the warehouse must be clearly marked to allow workers to find inventory quickly and efficiently. Just as houses have addresses, inventory locations have addresses identifying where the items are kept. A typical address includes the building number, aisle number, bay and level. They may even go into more detail and include information such as shelf and drawer numbers for smaller items. Often these labels are bar coded to allow automated recording when inventory is stocked or removed from a certain location.

Reverse Logistics

What is Reverse Logistics?

Reverse logistics is a complete supply chain dedicated to the reverse flow of products and materials for the purpose of returns, repairs, remanufacture and/or recycling. When a customer returns an item to a retail outlet, or if another customer in the supply chain rejects a shipment due to damages, it begins the process of reverse logistics. Often, it is the warehouse or distribution center and its personnel that must bear the responsibility and cost associated with this returned merchandise. It can cause a significant burden on both the workforce and the company if not managed properly.

In the United States, the total costs associated with reverse logistics are exceed $650 billion per year. That much volume encourages companies to streamline the process as much as possible. Needless to say, a range of technologies from bar codes to inventory management software are critical to improving the reverse logistics process.

There are two primary types of reverse logistics: the return of products; and ongoing practices such as recycling, and disposal of packaging and waste. Frontline material handling workers are impacted by both.

Product Returns

Historically, companies have focused primarily on the forward flow of logistics, selling and distributing goods. In recent decades, however, the impact of reverse logistics through product returns has become increasingly important, especially in e-commerce where returns are more than triple those for brick-and-mortar purchases.

Goods may be returned for many reasons, such as:

- Poor product quality.

- Damaged or defective products.

- Unneeded inventories resulting from over-forecast demand.

- Seasonal inventories.

- Out-of-date inventories.

- Remanufacturing and refurbishment of products.

CHAPTER 5

Terms To Know

Material Requirements Planning (MRP)

A set of techniques that uses bill of material (BOM) data, inventory data, and the master production schedule to calculate requirements for materials. It makes recommendations to release replenishment orders for material. Further, because it is time-phased, it makes recommendations to reschedule open orders when due dates and need dates are not in phase.

Time-phased MRP begins with the items listed on the MPS (master production schedule) and determines:

1. The quantity of all components and materials required to fabricate those items and

2. The date that the components and material are required. Time-phased MRP is accomplished by exploding the BOM bill of material, adjusting for inventory quantities on hand or on order, and offsetting the net requirements by the appropriate lead times.

Raw Material Stock

Purchased items or extracted materials that are converted via the manufacturing process into components and products.

Reverse Logistics

A complete supply chain dedicated to the reverse flow of products and materials for the purpose of returns, repair, remanufacture and/or recycling.

Warehouse Management System (WMS)

A system that manages all processes that a warehouse carries out. These processes include receiving, picking and shipping.

This function is sometimes done by a separate department because it often involves physical inspection of the product and other special handling procedures that are outside the handling of regular items. After inspection, the items can usually be returned to stock and controlled within regular inventory. If there is any damage it must be recorded and handled according to company policy.

If items are returned because they are damaged or defective, there are different options depending on the type of product and extent of damage or defect. Some damaged products can be salvaged and refurbished for future sale. Others may be usable for parts. Still other damaged goods may not be salvageable and must be discarded or destroyed.

There is a growing tendency in large operations to have a separate facility for handling returned goods.

Returned goods can be handled in different ways, such as:

• Returned to inventory

• Refurbished for resale

• Sold to alternate markets

• Broken down into reusable components

• Sorted to recover valuable materials

Due to the diverse ways and reasons for which products may be returned, reverse logistics is not as easily automated as forward logistics operations. However, most large distribution operations have automated the process where possible.

All items must be identified, tracked, reported and sorted for processing. Some products may be discarded and require no further tracking other than noting their disposal in the WMS. Other products may require manual inspection or even repair and refurbishment before they can enter into physical inventory. All of these actions must be recorded and tracked. Finally, credits may be issued to customers for the returned items.

Frontline material handling workers are not typically involved in the financial aspect of the transaction, but may be required to:

• Inspect returned merchandise

• Enter information about the merchandise into the WMS

• Stage returned items for storage, if applicable

• Dispose of damaged items properly

Sustainable Practices in Reverse Logistics

Recycling and reuse are two of the largest areas of reverse logistics due to ever increasing emphasis on environmental regulations and company efforts to reduce costs and improve efficiency. Waste management has become a multimillion-dollar industry, and many companies seek to reduce waste before it is even generated. For example, companies may seek to reduce the amount of packaging materials used in shipment of goods to reduce the amount of materials that must be disposed or recycled later.

Frontline workers may be involved in many aspects of this type of reverse logistics. Indeed, there are entire facilities and third-party companies devoted to the handling and transport of materials for recycling or reuse. Within regular logistics operations, frontline workers may be required to perform tasks related to sustainable reverse logistics, such as:

• Separating waste materials for recycling

• Handling returned merchandise

• Segregating returned items for reuse, as appropriate

• Reporting data related to recycling, reuse and waste management

• Processing and tracking reusable packaging materials such as plastic bins or pallets

Terms To Know

Work-in-Process (WIP)

A good or goods in various stages of completion throughout the plant, including all material from raw material that has been released for initial processing up to completely processed material awaiting final inspection and acceptance as finished goods inventory. Many accounting systems also include the value of semi-finished stock and components in this category.

CHAPTER 6

CHAPTER 6

Safe Handling of Hazardous Materials

Overview of Chapter

The purpose of this chapter is to explain how hazardous materials are handled. Almost every frontline material handler will have some contact with hazardous materials even if it is only the batteries of a forklift. These materials require special attention and care. This chapter will provide an overview of the various types of hazardous materials and the rules and regulations that govern their handling and transport.

Objectives

When you have completed this chapter, you will be able to do these things:

1. List government regulations related to hazmat handling.

2. Identify safe work practices for unloading and loading hazmats.

3. List government and other safe work practices for transfer and storage of hazmats.

4. Describe how hazmats are identified in shipping documentation.

Government Regulations

According to the U.S. Department of Transportation (USDOT), a hazardous material (hazmat) is a substance or material that is capable of posing an unreasonable risk to health, safety and property when transported in commerce. The USDOT is the primary agency responsible for developing and enforcing rules and regulations regarding the transport of hazmats. This authority is delegated to the Federal Aviation Administration (FAA), Federal Motor Carrier Safety Administration (FMCSA), Federal Railway Administration (FRA), Pipeline and Hazardous Materials Safety Administration (PHMSA), and the United States Coast Guard (USCG).

The Occupational Safety and Health Administration (OSHA), via the Hazard Communication Standard (HCS), also known as the Right-to-Know law, provides additional regulations regarding the handling and storage of hazmats. Hazard Communication (HAZCOM) is based on the idea that every worker has the right to know the dangers of the materials they are exposed to at work.

The law requires employers to tell employees about the dangers of hazmats and what they can do to protect themselves—before they begin working.

HCS is now aligned with the Globally Harmonized System of Classification and Labeling of Chemicals (GHS). GHS affects container labels that warn of potentially dangerous hazards. GHS also affects Safety Data Sheets (SDS). In the coming months and years, all workers will encounter more and more elements of the GHS. SDS will now be referred to as Data Sheet (SDS). SDS, similar to SDS, provides in depth information about the chemicals and products that workers work with.

According to OSHA, "the revised standards improve the quality and consistency of hazard information in the workplace, making it safer for workers by providing easily understandable information on appropriate handling and safe use of hazardous chemicals." The GHS has been adopted by a large number of nations, which reduces trade barriers and provides cost savings for businesses that regularly handle, store and use hazardous chemicals.

Hazmat Employees

A hazmat employee is any worker who directly affects the safe transportation of hazardous materials. This includes any employee responsible for loading and unloading hazmats, marking hazmat containers or packaging, preparing hazmats for transport, or transporting of hazmats. Current regulations require that all hazmat employees must be trained and certified and receive refresher training every three years. New employees must be trained within 90 days of their hire.

There are four basic elements of training required by USDOT:

- **General awareness training.** This is basic training that familiarizes employees with hazmat classifications, packaging, marking, labeling, documentation and placarding (use of a poster or sign that measures 10 ¾ x 10 ¾ inches placed on the outside of a container or vehicle to warn that a hazmat is inside the vehicle or container).

- **Function-specific training.** It is designed according to the specific task the employee will perform.

- **Safety training.** This training is required for all employees who actually handle hazmats and includes emergency response, protective measures and accident avoidance.

- **Driver training.** Drivers who transport hazmats are required to undergo special training. And, if the hazmat being transported requires placarding, then the driver must have a hazmat-endorsed Commercial Driver's License (CDL).

CHAPTER 6

Did You Know?

Responsibilities of Hazmat Shippers

- Determine whether a material meets the definition of a hazardous material
- Proper shipping name
- Class/division
- Identification number
- Hazard warning label
- Packaging
- Marking
- Employee training
- Shipping papers
- Emergency response information
- Emergency response telephone number
- Certification
- Compatibility
- Blocking and bracing
- Placarding
- Security plan
- Incident reporting

Global Harmonization Standard

GHS is a system for standardizing and harmonizing the classification and labeling of chemicals. It is a logical and comprehensive approach to:

- Defining health, physical, and end environmental hazards of chemicals.

- Creating classification processes that use available data on chemicals for comparison with the defined hazard criteria.

- Communicating hazard information, as well as protective measures, on labels and Safety Data Sheets (SDS).

The GHS is not a regulation or standard. It establishes agreed hazard classification and communications provisions with explanatory information on how to apply the system. The production and use of chemicals is fundamental to all economies. Every country has its own system of regulations regarding the production, use and transportation of hazardous materials. Many have different definitions of what is hazardous, how much of a certain chemical constitutes a hazard, etc. With ever increasing global trade, these differences significantly impact trade and commerce.

Hazmat Classification

Hazmats are categorized into nine classes based on characteristics or specific hazards presented. They are:

- Class 1: Explosives

- Class 2: Gases (Flammable, Non-flammable and Toxic)

- Class 3: Liquids (Flammable and Combustible)

- Class 4: Flammable Solids, Spontaneously Combustible, and Dangerous When Wet

- Class 5: Oxidizers and Organic Peroxides

- Class 6: Poison (Toxic), Poison Inhalation Hazard and Infectious Substance

- Class 7: Radioactive Materials

- Class 8: Corrosive Materials

- Class 9: Other Dangerous Goods or Hazardous Materials

Labeling

Hazmats that are not stored or transported in bulk must be individually labeled. Basic requirements are that the label:

- Includes the class number at the bottom of the label

- Includes the material symbol at the top of the label

- Must be located on the same surface and near the PSN (Proper Shipping Name)

- Must be clearly visible

- Must be weather resistant

- Cannot be covered by any other label or markings

General Guidelines

Hazmats must be handled with extreme caution. Certain steps need to be taken to ensure safety not only for the hazmat handlers, but also for co-workers, equipment and the environment. There are different types of hazmats (solids, liquids, gases, powders), and while each class has special requirements, there are general guidelines that help workers stay safe when working with these dangerous substances.

General safety. Only trained employees should handle hazmats. Read all labels and directions before handling hazmats. Know what materials are being handled, their potential dangers and general emergency response information.

Protective gear. Avoid direct contact with the materials and their containers by wearing protective clothing such as gloves, hazmat suits and boots. Avoid breathing hazardous fumes with a mask or respirator. Wear safety goggles for eye protection. Always wash

hands thoroughly after handling any hazardous substance. Dispose of protective gear in the proper receptacles to avoid contamination.

Work environment. When handling solvents, toxic gases or other noxious hazmats, make sure that the area is well ventilated and avoid long exposure.

Loading and Unloading Hazmats

Special care must be taken when loading and unloading hazardous materials. Each mode of transportation has unique rules. The basic precautions, however, are the same.

General Rules

- Make sure that packages are secure against movement in the vehicle. Hazmats must be protected against sudden movement.

- No smoking is allowed near any flammable substance.

- There should be no open flames near the loading/unloading zone.

- The truck or trailer must be secured (handbrake set, chocks in place, etc.)

CHAPTER 6

Terms To Know

Basic Description

Required description on documentation when shipping or handling hazmats. It must include: the Identification Number; Proper Shipping Name; Hazard Class or Division; and Packing Group (if applicable).

Bonding

A system that connects various pieces of conductive equipment together to keep them at the same potential. Static sparking cannot take place between objects that are the same potential.

Corrosives

Materials that can attack and chemically destroy exposed body tissues. Corrosives can also damage or even destroy metal. They begin to cause damage as soon as they touch the skin, eyes, respiratory tract, digestive tract, or the metal.

Grounding

A special form of bonding in which conductive equipment is connected to an earthing electrode or to the building grounding system to prevent sparking between conductive equipment and grounded structures.

Hazardous Material

Hazardous material (hazmat) defined by environmental laws and legal precedents. A product has been defined as hazardous by regulations that impose stiff fines if the regulations are ignored.

- Use caution with tools and equipment. Take care not to puncture packaging or containers during loading and unloading.

- A qualified person must be present at all times during cargo tank loading and unloading.

- When handling flammables and explosives, proper grounding should be established to prevent static electric charges from igniting the substance.

Specific Requirements by Class

Class 1 (Explosives)

- Stop engine.

- Use proper caution (avoid hooks, sharps, throwing, dropping, and keep away from hot exhaust pipes).

Class 2 (Gases)

- Floors and platforms must be essentially flat or loaded onto suitable racks.

- Stop engine unless using a pump powered by the vehicle to load or unload.

- Cargo tank liquid discharge valves must be closed and free of leaks.

- Discharge control procedures for emergencies must be written and carried on the motor vehicle when transporting liquefied compressed gases.

- A safety check before unloading must be performed by the qualified person to ensure the hoses, valves, fittings, etc. are suitable and safe for unloading.

- An emergency shutdown must be accomplished by the authorized person if there is a leak during unloading.

- Check the remote shut-off device daily.

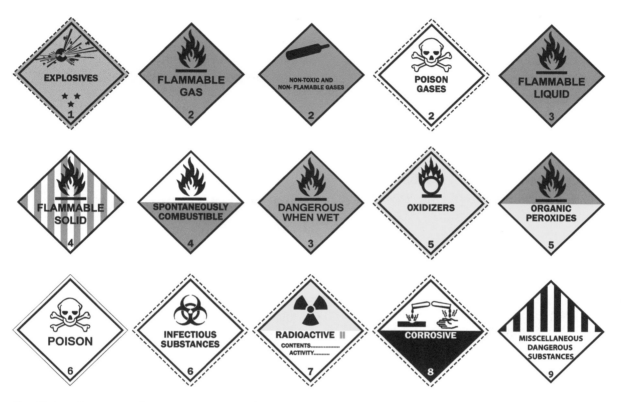

Facilities that store hazmats are required to post signs warning of the possible dangers.

Class 3 (Flammable Liquids)

- Stop engine.

- All containers must be bonded and grounded.

- A qualified person must attend to combustible liquids in cargo tanks. The worker must remain within 150 feet of the cargo tank and 25 feet of the delivery hose, and also must observe the hose and the cargo tank at least once every five minutes.

Class 4 (Flammable Solids) & Class 5 (Oxidizer and Organic Peroxides):

- All loading must be within the body of the vehicle and covered.

- Articles must be kept dry.

- A spontaneous combustion hazard must be assured of sufficient ventilation if known by the carrier.

- Nitrates require special handling such as having floors swept clean, having no projections or sharp objects that could cut the bags, having suitable covering, etc.

- Smokeless powder for small arms cannot exceed 100 pounds per motor vehicle.

- Pyrophoric liquids in a cylinder must be loaded so that the valves are in the vapor space and all the cylinders are suitably secured.

CHAPTER 6

Class 6 (Poisonous) & Class 2 (Poison Gas)

- Arsenical compounds in bulk must be in water-tight, dust-tight, slit-proof hopper or dump-type vehicles.

- Use of interconnecting packages is not allowed.

- No foodstuffs, feed or edible food may be loaded with a package bearing the "POISON" or "POISON INHALATION HAZARD" label.

- No poison may be in the driver's compartment.

Class 7 (Radioactive):

- Load to avoid spillage.

- Load must be blocked and braced.

- Persons should not remain in vehicle unnecessarily.

Class 8 (Corrosive)

- Nitric acid of 50 percent or greater may not be loaded above any other package.

- Storage batteries must be loaded such that all batteries will be protected against other loading falling onto or against them, and they must be protected to prevent short circuits.

Storage and Transport of Hazmats

Storage

Storage containers and facilities must be well suited to the materials being stored in them. Certain substances may react with some types of containers, which could cause containment failure. Storage guidelines can differ based on different quantities of a substance. Federal requirements are based on reportable quantities (RQs), which means that the amount

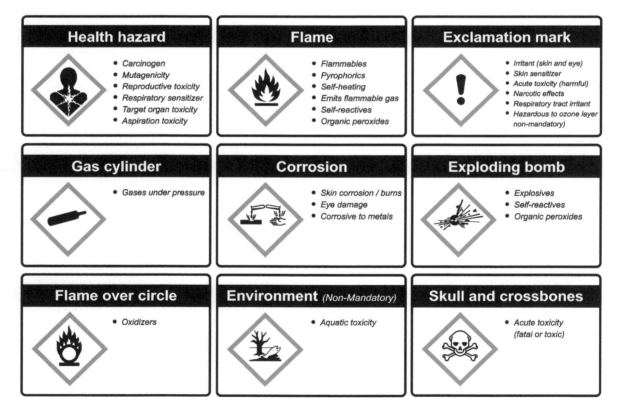

Storage guidelines can differ based on different quantities of a substance.

of the material exceeds threshold amounts specified by the government.

Containers

Hazardous materials must be stored in USDOT- approved containers with proper labeling. The Environmental Protection Agency (EPA) and USDOT also require secondary containment for hazmats, such as metal or plastic spill pallets or a dike area around buildings containing hazmats. This secondary containment must be large enough to contain 100 percent of the largest unit or 10 percent of the total of all units, whichever is larger. A container holding flammable materials must be kept away from sparks and flames.

Signs

Facilities that store hazmats are required to post signs warning of the possible dangers. The location where hazmats are stored must be clearly marked, and a Safety Data Sheet (SDS) must be posted in the area. "No Smoking" signs should be placed in an area where flammable materials are kept to reduce risks.

Terms To Know

Hazard Communication (HAZCOM)
Also known as the Right-to-Know law. HAZCOM is based on the idea that every worker has the right to know the dangers of the materials they are exposed to at work. The law requires employers to tell employees about the dangers of hazmats and what they can do to protect themselves—before they begin working.

Hazmat Employee
Any worker who directly affects the safe transportation of hazardous materials.

Safety Data Sheet (SDS)
A document intended to provide workers and emergency personnel with procedures for handling or working with that substance in a safe manner, and includes information such as physical data (melting point, boiling point, flash point, etc.), toxicity, health effects, first aid, reactivity, storage, disposal, protective equipment, and spill-handling procedures.

Oxidizer
A substance that oxidizes another substance, especially one that supports the combustion of fuel; an oxidizing agent.

Placard
A poster or sign that measures 10 ¾ x 10 ¾ inches placed on the outside of a container or vehicle to warn that a hazmat is inside the vehicle or container.

Placarding
Use of a poster or sign that measures 10 ¾ x 10 ¾ inches placed on the outside of a container or vehicle to warn that a hazmat is inside the vehicle or container.

Reportable Quantity (RQ)
The minimum quantity of a hazardous substance which, if released, is required to be reported.

CHAPTER 6

Elements of Safety Data Sheets (SDS)

A 16-section format SDS is used for chemicals used or stored within the work area. Employers must maintain copies of all SDS. The 16 sections are:

1. Identification
2. Hazard(s) identification
3. Composition/information on ingredients
4. First-aid measures
5. Fire-fighting measures
6. Accidental release measures
7. Handling and storage
8. Exposure controls/Personal protection
9. Physical and chemical properties
10. Stability and reactivity
11. Toxicological information
12. Ecological information
13. Disposal consideration
14. Transport information
15. Regulatory information
16. Other information including date or preparation of last revision

Environment

Facilities should be well ventilated. Temperatures must be controlled to avoid combustion, venting or container damage. Inside storage must have self-closing fire doors.

Transport

Transporting hazardous materials is highly regulated. Any shipper or transporter of hazmats that require placarding must register with the USDOT and pay a fee of $100 to

$1000. A Certificate of Registration is good for one year and must be renewed annually. A copy of the certificate must be on all vehicles used to transport hazmats.

When a vehicle is transporting hazmats, it must display certain warnings and labels notifying the public of the contents.

Permits

FMCSA requires carriers to obtain a Federal Safety Permit for certain hazmats transported above threshold amounts. This includes all radioactive materials, more than 55 pounds of explosives, toxic- by-inhalation substances and liquefied natural gas.

To obtain the permit, motor carriers must have a "satisfactory" safety rating; cannot have a crash rate in the top 30 percent of the national average; must certify that they have security and emergency communication plans in place; and ensure that they are in compliance with hazmat registration provisions.

Placarding

Vehicles that transport hazardous materials must be well marked according to specific USDOT guidelines. Placards must be placed on all four sides of the vehicle. As noted earlier, a placard is a poster or sign that measures 10 ¾ x 10 ¾ inches and is placed on the outside of a container or vehicle to warn that an HM is inside the vehicle or container. The placard must contain the hazard class, and it must be posted away from other markings or labels on the vehicle.

Hazmat Documentation

Every aspect of hazmat handling is regulated including shipping papers, marking, labeling and packaging. Even for non-certified hazmat employees, it is important to be able to identify hazardous materials on shipping papers and other transport documentation. Government requirements for hazmat documentation make this relatively easy.

Shipping papers

Hazardous materials must be identified in the shipping paper in one of three ways:

- Listed on a separate hazmat shipping paper.

- Listed in a sharply contrasting color or highlighted.

- Have an "X" in an "HM" (or hazmat) column on the paper.

The shipping paper must include the "Basic Description" of the material. The government also regulates this description. It must meet certain requirements and include specific information in a particular order.

The hazmat description must meet the following requirements:

- Be in English.

- Be legible: printed by hand or mechanically.

- No abbreviations (except those specifically allowed in the regulations).

- Not interrupted by additional information such as phone numbers, addresses, etc.

The description must include the following information in the order listed below:

- The Proper Shipping Name (PSN).

- The hazard class.

- The identification number.

- The packaging group (PG).

For example:

Emergency Information

The shipping papers must also include basic emergency response information including at least the following information:

- The basic description.

- Immediate health hazards.

- Fire or explosion risks.

- Immediate precautions to be taken in the event of an incident.

- Initial methods for handling spills or leaks.

- Preliminary first aid information.

Companies that provide shipping papers to carriers are required to retain copies of those papers for two years. Carriers are required to keep the shipping paper for one year. For hazardous waste shipments both the person providing the shipping paper and the carrier must retain the shipping paper for three years.

PSN	Class	ID #	PG
Benzoquinone	6.1	UN2587	II

CHAPTER 7

Evaluation of Transportation Modes (Truck, Air, Rail, Water)

Overview of Chapter

The purpose of this chapter is to explain the various modes of transportation and how they are used throughout the supply chain. Each mode of transportation has its own function in the supply chain. This chapter will describe the value of each mode and the criteria used to evaluate transportation effectiveness and efficiency.

Objectives

When you have completed this chapter, you will be able to do these things:

1. Describe each mode of transportation and its advantages and disadvantages.

2. List the main considerations in determining the best mode of transportation to use.

3. Explain how to use the information on performance of the different modes for rapid decision making.

4. Give examples of transportation documentation.

Transportation Modes: Advantages & Disadvantages

Truck

Within the United States, most products are transported by trucks on public roadways. Trucking allows pick-up and delivery between any two points served by roads. There are several modes of truck delivery: common, contract, line haul, express and private fleet carriers. Each of these carrier types serves a different but very important role in the distribution cycle. A typical trailer of finished products normally weighs approximately 50,000 to 55,000 pounds. In some states however, they allow trailers to be pulled in tandem making the load around 100,000 pounds.

The various truck receiving activities at warehouses and distribution centers are determined by the type of operation. These activities include: yard control, vendor delivery truck or container dock scheduling, unloading product into the inbound staging area, verifying the product quality and quantity, entering receipts into inventory, identifying the product and transporting the product to the storage area.

Yard control or inbound dock scheduling determines the time that the delivery truck is allowed at an unloading dock. Trailer yard movement and control are a very important function for larger operations, sometimes moving hundreds of trailers per day in and out of available doors. Some large distribution centers use what are commonly referred to as yard jockeys who do nothing but spot trailers all day or night.

In some operations, the yard driver is responsible for chocking trailers after they have been moved to the door. However, it should be understood that it is still the unloader's responsibility to check that the trailer is secured one way or another before beginning the unloading process. Other yard duties include checking the seal, opening the truck door and visually inspecting the trailer or load condition for any obvious or external damage.

Advantages. Trucks are well suited for moving a small volume of goods to many destinations. Additionally, trucks can usually deliver freight in less time than other modes for shipments shorter than 500 miles. They can be loaded before the actual transportation begins.

Trucks can be owned or leased, but the vehicle costs are low compared to air, sea and rail. As long as the roads are in good condition, trucks provide fast, flexible service. Trucks also allow the internal environment of the trailer to be controlled (refrigerated or heated) to protect goods, especially food products.

Disadvantages. Trucks must pay substantial fuel, license fees and tolls. These costs vary by the load (with a truckload being up to 100,000 pounds). Fleet vehicles require additional in-house routing and scheduling work. Refrigerated (reefer) and heated trucks may require additional power while being loaded or stored at a dock.

Air

Air freight is a major player in international supply chain logistics. Air transport is often used for low-weight, high-value products such as electronics and jewelry. For such items, the

Fast Facts: Trucks

Trucks move more than 70% of the nation's freight by weight.

Gross freight revenues from trucking exceed $730 billion annually.

About 38 million trucks are registered and used for business.

All registered trucks travel more than 300 billion miles annually, consuming 45 million gallons of fuel.

There are roughly 1 million private carrier firms on file with the Federal Motor Carrier Safety Administration.

Nearly 3.4 million truck drivers on the job, with annual turnover of 99%.

CHAPTER 7

Fast Facts: Water

The seaborne international shipping industry moves about 90% of the world's goods.

Goods moved ships range from bulk materials such as iron ore and oil plus a range of finished goods from electronic equipment to apparel.

There are more than 500,000 merchant ships registered in 150 nations carrying freight.

About 11 billion tons of freight move annually by large ship.

The five busiest ports in the U.S. (in descending order) are: Port of Los Angeles; Port of Long Beach; Port of New York and New Jersey; Georgia Ports; Port of Seattle and Tacoma.

These five ports handle more than 32 million TEUs annually.

The inland waterways of the U.S. include more than 25,000 miles of navigable waters.

cost of air shipment is small compared with the value of the product.

Air shipment is also used for emergency deliveries. Essential repair parts are often shipped by air.

There are a number of methods that material movers use to ship via air freight in the supply chain. One is to tender the freight directly to an airline. This can be done through an all-cargo airline, such as FedEx, UPS and DHL or with passenger airlines with air cargo divisions such as American Airlines or Delta.

In addition, Amazon has its own air cargo airline known as Amazon Air. It ships exclusively Amazon packages unlike other air cargo services that deliver for a broad range of shippers.

Advantages. Air transport is the fastest way to move products, especially over long distances or overseas. Combined with local ground transport, air transport can deliver products within a day anywhere in the United States and much of the world. The main advantage of air transport is speed. Air cargo service is also flexible provided there is a suitable landing strip.

Disadvantages. Airplanes are the most expensive type of transportation to operate. They have high fuel and maintenance costs. The disadvantage of shipping via air is that it is the most expensive option and is limited based on the physical characteristics of the goods shipped. Air carriers bear heavy fixed and variable costs (e.g., owning or leasing aircraft, operating cargo terminals and maintenance facilities, paying user fees for airports and air traffic control).

To determine the most competitive pricing for international air freight, international freight forwarders are often the main point of contact.

Rail

Railroads run only where there is a large market for heavy-volume shipping. Railways move large volumes of heavy bulk products such as coal, chemicals, autos and grain, over long distances. Each railcar can carry about twice the load weight of a truck, and a single train may have a hundred railcars. For most rail carriers, the number two volume commodity after coal is intermodal truck trailers.

Advantages. Railroads are best suited to move large volumes of bulky goods over long distances, which make them highly cost efficient. Trainloads can be made up of 100 cars each with a carrying capacity in the order of 160,000 pounds. Their speed is good over long distances, and they can carry a wide variety of goods. Rail works well combined with other modes by "piggyback" operations such as TOFC (trailer-on- flatcar) and COFC (containers-on-flatcar).

Disadvantages. Trains do not leave as often as trucks and are limited to locations served by rail lines. Since the infrastructure costs of rail transport are high, trains also require large orders to be cost effective. More delivery time (as much as 10 days within the U.S.) must be allocated.

Water

Water-borne transport includes oceangoing, coastal and inland vessels. This mode is used primarily to transport large or bulky materials over long distances.

Inland waterways are used to transport products such as coal, petroleum and iron ore. Farm products and wood are also transported this way in bulk. Examples of inland transport within the U.S. are lake freighters on the Great Lakes and barges on the Mississippi and Ohio rivers and inter-coastal waterways.

About 90% of all import merchandise comes into the U.S. via ocean container. For this reason, it is normal for inbound port cities to

Fast Facts: Air

Air cargo is focused mostly on movement of high-value goods for which delivery within a few hours is often critical.

A large cargo plane can carry as much cargo as roughly five truck containers.

Globally, more than 60 million tons of freight are moved by commercial airlines annually.

There are nearly 900 planes in the U.S. air cargo fleet.

The largest flow of air cargo is between East Asia and the U.S.

The five largest air cargo hubs in the U.S. (in descending order) are: Memphis, TN; Anchorage, AK; Louisville, KY; Los Angeles, CA; Miami, FL.

CHAPTER 7

have large break/bulk distribution centers that break down those shipments for re-distribution to warehouses around the country.

Ocean freight carriers are those companies that actually own and operate ocean-going vessels. There are four primary types of cargo vessels:

- Container ships – The freight is stowed in either 20-feet or 40-feet weather-tight ocean containers (20-feet and 40-feet are the most common size of containers).

Fast Facts: Pipeline

The U.S. has more petroleum pipelines than any other nation.

Pipelines range in diameter from 2 inches to 4 feet.

In the U.S., about 3 million miles of pipelines deliver trillions of cubic feet of natural gas and billions of tons of liquid petroleum.

It would take 750 tanker trucks loading up every 2-1/2 minutes and operating 24/7 to equal the volume moved by a modes sized pipeline.

- Bulk carriers – The most common is the tanker which moves bulk liquid cargo such as crude oil.

- Ro-Ro vessels – Roll-on/Roll-Off ships where motorized cargo such as automobiles, construction machinery or trucks is driven on and off ships.

- Break-bulk – Ships that accommodate dry goods too large to stow in a container.

Advantages. Ships and barges have a much larger capacity than trucks, railcars and cargo planes. One barge has the capacity of approximately 15 rail cars or 60 tractor trailers. Water transport is reliable and cost-effective. For example, on a ton-mile basis, rail costs are approximately twice as high as inland water carriers, whereas truck costs are approximately 20 times higher than inland water carriers.

Disadvantages. Water is a slow means of moving product. Inland barges travel approximately six miles per hour. Typical ocean transport time from the U.S. West Coast to the Pacific Rim is 14 days and longer. The transit time from the U.S. East Coast to Europe is about 10-12 days.

Pipelines

Pipelines move only gas, oil and refined products. Capital costs for pipelines are high and are borne by the carrier, but operating costs are very low.

In sum, each of the five modes of transportation has some advantages over the other modes of transportation. Attractiveness depends on a combined calculation of cost, speed, reliability, capability, capacity and flexibility. Keep in mind that a mode's performance is also dependent on quality of its supporting infrastructure: roads, airports, ports, canals, rivers and coastal mains.

Intermodal Shipping

Intermodal shipping involves using multiple transportation modes to move products to consumers in the most cost-effective and secure manner. In an increasingly global economy, multiple modes are used to transport a shipment from its origin to its destination without the contents being reloaded or disturbed.

Intermodal transportation occurs when two or more modes work closely together in an attempt to utilize the advantages of each mode while at the same time minimizing their disadvantages. For example, a company might use piggyback transportation, that is, either truck trailer-on-flatcar or container-on-flatcar, to take advantage of rail's low transportation costs on the line-haul along with truck's ability to provide door-to-door service. Intermodal shipping will be discussed in greater detail in Chapter 8.

Considerations in Determining the Best Mode

Efficient transportation is the physical movement of goods and people between two points, and it is vital for successful supply chain operations. Decisions about the most effective modes of transportation are made primarily by traffic managers and clerks in distribution operations, freight forwarding companies and by dispatch and tracking personnel within transportation companies.

Material handling personnel should be aware of the basic considerations involved in selecting transportation modes for any given shipment. The transportation mode selected affects the packaging required, and carrier classification rules dictate package choice. The type of carrier used can determine material handling

Fast Facts: Rail

The entire U.S. rail network is 155,300 miles.

Eighty percent of the U.S. rail network is used for freight.

About 700 railroad companies operate common carrier freight service operations.

The volume of goods transported by rail in the U.S. is 1.6 trillion ton miles.

There are more than 26,500 Class 1 rail locomotives.

The rail industry adds more than $45 billion to the U.S. economy annually.

Railroad operations and capital investment support more than 1.1 million jobs.

equipment needs and the design of receiving and shipping docks.

A major consideration involved in selecting any mode is cost. Transportation is the most expensive logistics activity, representing over 40 percent of most corporations' logistics expenses. Transportation expenses are rising faster than other logistics costs due to smaller, more frequent orders, increased international trade and global logistics, rising fuel costs, labor shortages, less carrier competition due to carrier mergers and acquisitions, and increased labor rates.

There are many factors that impact total transportation costs: freight, fleet, fuel, maintenance, labor, insurance, pick-up and delivery, loading and unloading costs, terminal handling, time when a transport vehicle is idle, billing and collecting, taxes and tolls, and international fees.

The cost of transportation is also affected by the location of a firm's plants, warehouses, vendors, retail locations and customers. Being able to combine the largest number of shipments can help lower costs by taking advantage of volume discounts. However, the need for customer service may also affect choice of carrier.

Transport costs include fixed costs which do not change with the amount or volume or goods carried.

The cost of a truck is a fixed cost. Variable costs are costs of operation which depend on fuel, maintenance, labor and how the loads are handled (one load per truck or many).

Various measures can be used to reduce costs. For example, a shipper can work to:

- Increase the weight shipped

- Reduce the number of pick-ups

Did you Know?

Containerization

The widespread adoption of standardized intermodal containers in the 1960s revolutionized the logistics industry. With an international standard for the size, connectivity and capacity of containers, companies can transport goods via more than one transportation mode without the products being unloaded and reloaded onto a different piece of equipment.

Containers arriving on a ship in Long Beach, CA can be put directly on a train bound for Ft. Worth, TX. Once they arrive in Texas a few days or a week later, the containers can be put onto trucks for regional delivery.

During the process, the container does not have to be opened and the materials inside are never handled individually until they arrive at the final distribution or wholesale facility where they are opened and unloaded for distribution.

Prior to containerization, the above scenario would have taken considerably longer because the items would have often required individual handling between each mode of transport: removed in unit loads from the ship and put onto a train car, then unit loads moved from the train car to a truck trailer, and finally, unit loads moved from the truck to a distribution center where they would be broken into individual cases or boxes. This process may have taken days or weeks longer than today's more streamlined effort.

- Decrease the number of parcels by consolidating shipments

- Decrease billing and collecting costs by consolidating shipments

At the same time, the best transportation solution must not overwhelm the vehicle, the container, the workforce capacities or lane capacities. Lane capacities also set limits on how fast or how often the shipments can take place.

Legal Forms of Transportation

In dealing with transportation carriers, it is useful to be aware that they are also organized into categories for legal purposes. Commonly used terms include:

- **Common carriers.** These accept responsibility for carrying goods at any time, to any place and for all shippers, usually at a set rate

- **Private carriers.** These are owned by the firms which produce the goods, so that shipment of these goods is not apportioned out to third parties.

- **Contract carriers.** These operate on a selective basis and may charge variable rates to customers based on negotiated terms.

Terms To Know

Common Carriers

Transportation available to the public that does not provide special treatment to any one party and is regulated as to the rates charged, the liability assumed, and the service provided. A common carrier must obtain a certificate of public convenience and necessity from the Federal Trade Commission for interstate traffic.

Containerization

A shipment method in which commodities are placed in containers, and after initial loading, the commodities per se are not re-handled in shipment until they are unloaded at the destination.

Contract Carriers

A carrier that does not serve the general public, but provides transportation for hire for one or a limited number of shippers under a specific contract.

Cross-Docking

The concept of packing products on the incoming shipments so they can be easily sorted at intermediate warehouses or for outgoing shipments based on final destination. The items are carried from the incoming vehicle docking point to the outgoing vehicle docking point without being stored in inventory at the warehouse. Cross-docking reduces inventory investment and storage space requirements.

- **Exempt carriers.** These are not regulated by federal and/or state mandates; carriage of fishing and agricultural products has been traditionally labeled exempt from regulatory practices.

- **Line-haul carriers.** These haul full loads long distances for one stop delivery in some cases to a "break/bulk" center where the product is then redistributed.

Carriers and Freight Forwarders

Carriers are usually associated with certain transportation modes and delivery specializations. Here are some well-known examples:

- Express/parcel carrier
- Less-than-truckload (LTL) trucking company
- Full truckload (FTL) trucking company
- Ocean liner
- Railroad
- Air Carrier/Integrator

In an increasingly global economy, most carriers are involved in intermodal transportation in one way or the other.

Freight forwarders are important participants in global supply chain logistics. They serve as intermediaries between the shipper and the carrier. Generally, they have large-scale relationships with both ocean freight and airfreight carriers.

Transportation Routes or Networks

Think of a route as the path along which products move. Networks are composed of paths and facilities connected by those paths. In selecting modes of transportation, it is important to be aware of the variety of practices and carriers along those paths that can best satisfy your needs for each stage of

Terms To Know

FTL vs LTL

What is the difference between FTL (full-truckload) and LTL (less-than-truckload) shipping?

FTL means that the load from one customer fills up the entire truck.

LTL means that the load from one customer does not take up the entire available space on the truck.

Shippers that accommodate full truck loads cater to customers who usually ship in bulk. The large amount of goods being shipped offsets the cost of the full truck.

For those shipping smaller items or items that do not fill an entire truck, an LTL shipment is the way to go. Most LTL loads average between 151 pounds and 10,000 pounds per load. With loads of more than 10,000 pounds it is often more cost effective to use FTL.

With an LTL shipment, the customer only pays for the amount of space used on the truck. For example, if the products only take up a quarter of the truck, the customer only pays for a quarter of the cost for the truck. The rest of the truck is packed with shipments from other companies that also want to save money on their smaller shipments.

These options are ideal for smaller businesses that do not ship in large volumes, like their larger counterparts.

Because of the nature of an LTL load, it can take longer than an FTL load to arrive at its destination. LTL loads typically have more destinations or pick-up locations to accommodate the different needs of the various shipments on board. The larger FTL loads usually contain a shipment for one company and one destination.

transportation. For example, containers can be decoupled, or separated from the truck tractors or railway engines. Being able to decouple gives more flexibility in routing, dispatching and temporary storage.

Another aspect of the selection process is "the mix". Each mode of transportation has its own mix of speed, cost, availability and capability. For example, speed can be traded for lower cost. It depends on what is being shipped and what attribute is most important.

There can also be different trade-offs within each mode. For example, in trucking, it is much cheaper to send full truckload (FTL) shipments than it is to use less-than-truckload (LTL) shipments, but using FTL shipments requires building up inventory and may delay shipments. Even when companies can manage to have full truck load (FTL) shipments, they still have to figure out what to do with the truck after it makes a delivery. They can do backhauls, which are shipments in the opposite direction, or they can send the truck to the nearest distribution center rather than returning to its origin.

FTL and LTL carriers can further be broken-up into two major categories: long-haul and short-haul.

Long-haul carriers generally serve most destinations within the lower-48 states. Short-haul carriers, on the other hand, have a service area within a specific geographic region (e.g., Northeast, Midwest or Southeast). Short-haul carriers are often referred to as regional carriers.

Shipping within a limited geographical region normally uses a single mode from source to destination. Intermodal transportation, which uses two or more modes, is used for longer

distances, such as in international trade. Intermodal shipments are usually shipped in steel cargo containers that can be transferred between specially fitted rail cars, container ships and tractor-trailers.

Shipments from Multiple Facilities

A special problem arises when orders require shipments from multiple facilities. The simplest solution is to coordinate them so that they arrive on the same day. However, this approach just transfers the cost of combining shipments to the customer, and many customers' object. The alternative is a merge in transit in which the multiple shipments are sent to a distribution

center near the customer site, reloaded onto a single truck and sent as a single delivery.

The most cost-effective way to do this is cross-docking, a technique in which goods are moved directly from a receiving dock to a shipping dock without intermediate storage.

Freight Forwarders

Freight forwarders buy large blocks of space on airlines to various locations. They pay for this space whether it is used or not. They also furnish pick-up and delivery arrangements, providing a door-to-door service for customers. They can offer considerable cost savings to the shipper. They also assist in choosing the right carrier for the shipment, in preparing documentation and notifying the consignee about the arrival of their shipment.

For international airfreight, the forwarder prepares the air waybill, based upon the information provided through a shipper's Letter of Instruction and other export documents. They may also submit the Shipper's Export Declaration data.

Integrated Carriers

FedEx, UPS and DHL are integrated carriers. They offer complete door-to-door service.

Next Flight Out Services

Next Flight Out (NFO) or counter-to-counter service is for critical shipments that must

be delivered the same day they are shipped. NFO shipments are usually with commercial passenger airlines. Generally, it is restricted to between 70 and 100 pounds per shipment. It must be at the airline approximately two hours before the flight departs to ensure it makes that flight. Many forwarders and integrators offer an NFO service.

Small Package Carriers

These carriers move packages ranging from a letter to 150 pounds. Depending upon the carrier, they can be moved either by ground or air. Ground services are cheaper than air services (per pound). Most small package carriers offer package insurance to the shipper. The first $100 of value is insured for free, but insurance costs for high value shipments can be quite expensive.

Expedited Carriers

Critical shipments that cannot be delivered on time using LTL carriers can be sent by expedited carriers that meet required delivery times cheaper than by air freight.

Time Definite

These are carriers that offer specialized equipment and precise pick-up and delivery time commitments that are guaranteed.

Specialty Carriers

Specialty carriers handle freight that requires special equipment. This may include bulk freight; large, difficult to handle freight; or freight requiring temperature controls such as refrigeration.

Refrigerated trailers are commonly known in the industry as reefers. Other commodities, such as some chemicals, require "protection from freezing" (PFF). For this type of service, heated trailers are necessary.

Measuring Quality

Transportation quality and reliability are as important, if not more important than cycle time, in selecting the most effective modes of transportation. A shipment delivered quickly to the wrong location or that arrives damaged is of no use. The following are common measures of transportation quality:

- Claims-free shipment percentage. The percentage of shipments without claims for each driver or carrier on each lane at each location.

- Damage-free shipment percentage. The percentage of shipments without damage for each driver or carrier on each lane at each location.

- Distance between accidents. The miles or kilometers between accidents for each driver, carrier and lane.

- On-time arrival percentage (OTAP). The percentage of shipments arriving on-time for each driver, carrier and lane.

- On-time departure percentage (OTDP). The percentage of loads departing on-time for each driver, carrier and lane.

- Perfect delivery percentage (PDP). The PDP measures the percentage of shipments delivered without defects, including damage, documentation, arrival time, arrival location, loss, accidents and claims of any kind for each delivery, driver, lane and carrier.

- Perfect Route Percentage (PRP). The percentage of routes or trips with a perfect delivery.

The following helps rate the time it takes for delivery or cycle time including:

Terms To Know

Decoupling
Creating independence between supply and use of material. Commonly denotes providing inventory between operations so that fluctuations in the production rate of the supplying operation do not constrain production or use rates of the next operation.

Exempt Carriers
A for-hire carrier that is free from economic regulation.

Fixed Costs
An expenditure that does not vary with the production volume; for example, rent, property tax, and salaries of certain personnel.

Freight Forwarders
The 'middle man' between the carrier and the organization shipping the product. Often combines smaller shipments to take advantage of lower bulk costs.

Full Truckload (FTL)
When the load from one customer fills up the whole truck.

Less Than Truckload (LTL)
Either a small shipment that does not fill the truck or a shipment of not enough weight to qualify for a truckload quantity (usually set at about 10,000 lbs) rate discount, offered to a general commodity trucker.

Private Carriers
A group that provides transportation exclusively within an organization.

Variable Costs
An operating cost that varies directly with a change of one unit in the production volume (e.g., direct materials consumed, sales commissions).

CHAPTER 7

- **In-transit time variability.** Point-to-point in-transit time variability by driver, carrier, land and location.

- **Vehicle load/unload time.** Vehicle loading and unloading times at each pick-up/delivery location by driver, carrier, lane and location.

- **Detention time.** Time spent waiting for loading or unloading times at each pick-up/delivery location due to dock congestion and/or delays by the shipper or the consignee.

- **Delayed in traffic time.** The time spent idling or at reduced speed due to traffic congestion for each driver, carrier, lane and pick-up/delivery location.

Transportation and Logistics Trade-Offs

Freight is never free. Transportation costs are easy to measure and are an easy target for cost cutting. Often, companies also see it as a non-value-add, necessary evil; the freight traffic manager is heavily pressured to cut freight expense. Yet cost cutting in transportation may increase costs elsewhere because lower cost carriers may provide poor service with

outdated equipment, poorly trained drivers and underinsurance.

Carriers should be part of the solution and not a source of problems. To make carriers part of the solution, shippers may select a limited number of carriers or core carriers to provide all company transportation needs. They may also seek to reducing complexity by using routing guides and working closely with a select few carriers as partners to the benefit of both.

Using Information on Different Modes

The maintenance and use of reliable data on various materials carriers can expedite and improve decisions on selecting transportation modes. Before selecting a specific type of vehicle, it is worth making a checklist of the requirements such as the ones set out in the following list:

- **Product characteristics:** Size; weight; unitization (what each unit consists of); susceptibility to damage, whether it is hazardous, frozen, liquid, powder; whether it has hygiene requirements such as food or live animals.

- **Method of loading or delivery:** By fork-lift truck; manual handling; overhead gantry (height limitation); straddle carrier (containers); from the side, rear, front, top or bottom (oil tankers).

- **Restrictions at the point of delivery or lading:** Narrow roads; low bridges; weight restrictions; night-time restrictions because of noise, lack of material handling equipment and low or limited building access.

- **Terrain to be covered:** Motorways or highways; urban roads; low-quality rural roads, lanes or graded roads; mountains or flatlands; and extreme heat or cold.

- **Fuel type:** Diesel; gasoline; liquefied petroleum gas (LPG); and natural gas, compressed natural gas (CNG) or liquefied natural gas (LNG).

- **Vehicle configuration:** Articulated tractor and trailer (truck part and trailer hooked together at a hinge); two-, three- or four-axle rigid vehicle; and a small goods vehicle.

- **Body types:** Curtain-sided; platform; skeletal suitable for carrying certain types of containers; van bodies; tankers; tipping body such as dump trucks; road-trailers suitable for transfer to rail wagons and bulk carriers.

- **Legal requirements:** Gross vehicle weight limits; vehicle dimensions; mandatory equipment; vehicle licenses; insurance requirements.

- **Vehicle economy:** Fuel consumption; tire wear; whole life costs; residual values; ease of maintenance.

- **Drivers' cab types:** Sleeper; day cab or crew carrier.

- **Additional equipment required:** Self-loading cranes; blower units; refrigeration units; fork-lifts carried with the vehicle; tail-lifts and fire extinguishers.

- **Vehicle security:** Locks; alarms; sealing devices; tracking devices using satellites, GSM (global system for mobile communications) or GPS (global positioning systems).

- **Vehicle restrictions:** Types and numbers of vehicles available and vehicle capacity.

- **Monitoring the vehicles:** Mileage traveled; tons carried; fuel used; and deliveries made.

Examples of Transportation Documentation

Vehicle/Container Identification, Tracking, and Communications

To track shipments in real time requires the ability to automatically identify, track and communicate with stationary and in-transit vehicles and containers. Technology in this area is advancing faster than in any other area of transportation management. The advances were motivated in part by the loss of thousands of Operation Desert Storm containers in the deserts of Kuwait.

To combat this problem, the Department of Defense began a program of Total Asset Visibility. One of the advances from that program was the use of bar coding, radio-frequency communication, radio-frequency tags and advanced global positioning systems for use in commercial transportation management. As long as each container has a bar code license plate, bar code scanners can be used to identify each container with handheld automatic scanners.

Containerization

The container is regarded as the key development in intermodal transportation since the 1970s. A container is a box that can range between 8-feet and 56-feet long. Containers can be moved seamlessly between water, rail and truck. Most containers are made of steel and are general purpose in nature, meaning they can carry any type of freight. Specialized intermodal containers that carry tanks for holding liquids or gases as well as containers that hold insulated or refrigerated cargo are also available.

Container ports are ports dedicated to receiving container ships. The containers are off-loaded from ships and sent out via rail or truck. Containers are moved by mechanical devices such as container cranes, and companies need only handle a container and not the freight inside it — thus providing a dramatic reduction in freight handling costs.

As a result, most shippers make use of containerized freight when possible. This transportation service is sold in full container loads (FCL) or in less than container loads (LCL). As in the case of truck freight, full loads cost less per pound or kilogram than less than full loads.

The international standard for containers is 20-feet and 40-feet which allows handling anywhere in the world. Modified 53-feet containers which are suited for road transportation are also common, and some container ships have been modified to accept these modified units.

Freight Documentation and Management

Freight management and associated freight documentation is one of the most profitable (if done properly) and expensive (if done poorly) parts of transportation management.

Freight rate negotiations are now more thorough and more carefully researched than ever. Shippers come to the negotiating table with documentation such as the following:

- Historical and projected shipping volumes.

- Required delivery times.

- Guidelines for claims and dispute resolution.

- Historical carrier performance records.

- Required information systems support capability.

- Preferred payment terms.

- Carrier's competitive position.

- Knowledge of carrier's customer base and competitive position.

Bills of lading, as described earlier, provide vital information on who is shipping what, where, and its characteristics. In addition, the primary document in ocean transport is the ocean bill of lading. It is similar to a motor freight bill of lading in purpose and most detail, but an ocean bill of lading may or may not be a negotiable instrument. In other words, physical possession of the original document may be required to take possession of the goods covered by the ocean bill of lading.

International transportation includes the import or the export of goods to or from a point between countries. Most often, distribution centers handle the import side of this activity. That is, of course, goods coming into one country from outside countries.

The primary difference, from an operational standpoint, between domestic and international transportation is the documentation requirements associated with international trade. When freight is coming into or leaving a country, certain documents are required to enable the freight to move effectively.

Notes

CHAPTER 8

Dispatch and Tracking Operations

Overview of Chapter

The purpose of this chapter is to explain dispatch and tracking of products as they are transported throughout the supply chain. Today, most products are shipped using more than one mode of transportation and often internationally. This chapter will describe how intermodal shipments and international transportation impact supply chain operations.

Objectives

When you have completed this chapter, you will be able to do these things:

1. Explain shipping documentation..

2. Describe the main factors related to vehicle routing.

3. List ways to track cargo within the yard.

4. List ways to track cargo en route.

5. Describe key features of intermodal transportation.

6. Describe basic customs terminology and documentation.

Shipping Documentation

Documentation is an important part of shipping operations. Accurate records ensure that the correct products are placed in the right vehicles for delivery.

Dispatch List / Shipping Schedule

Dispatching is the act of prioritizing all of the jobs related to shipping goods. A dispatch list is simply a list of those jobs in priority sequence. It is updated at least daily or at shift changes and usually includes the following information:

- Trailer loading schedule that includes what trailer arrives at what door.

- All of the orders that go on each trailer along with the appropriate paperwork.

- Any special shipments that are out of the norm (i.e., shipping equipment to another warehouse or distribution center).

- Express package pick-ups (FedEx, UPS).

Shipping Manifests

A manifest is a list of items in a vehicle's cargo. Different types of manifesting can be used depending upon the size of the operation. The manifest includes customer addresses, invoice numbers and package weights. It helps ensure that the right packages end up on the correct trailer.

- Manual manifests are handwritten lists in which an employee writes the package information onto the form. This is the most basic manifest document and is rarely used today.

• Two-part label manifests are computer-printed labels attached to the package exterior. Both sections of the label contain the same information. When the package is placed onto the vehicle, the driver tears off one section of the label which serves as the delivery record.

• Hand-held bar code manifesting uses bar code labels and hand-held scanners to record containers as they are loaded onto the vehicle. The scanners transmit the data to a computer where information is retained for the record. This type of manifesting is most commonly used by express package delivers such as FedEx, UPS and DHL and is less common for truckload carriers.

Load Weight Limits. In addition to ensuring that the proper packages are loaded onto the correct trailer, shipments must not exceed legal weight limits for the transport vehicle. Shipments are weighed and the information recorded on the shipping manifest to ensure that loads receive the proper transport fees and fall within legal limits.

First, packages or containers are weighed on scales. The weight is verified against the weight indicated on the container. The proper weight is then recorded on the shipping manifest. In most major centers, this function is handled by the transportation department through the use of computerized information.

Shipping Order

The shipping order is a document which specifies the products to be shipped, customer information and the mode of transport. The order includes the picking ticket list, and items are checked off the pick list ticket as they are packaged. It also includes any special requirements for packing and shipping.

Carrier Freight Bill

This is an invoice given to the shipper or consignee by the carrier as a request of payment for services. At a minimum it includes: the carrier's name, pro number, shipper's name and address, consignee's name and address, description of the goods, the rate charged, freight terms and total charges due.

Delivery Receipt (D/R)

This document is issued by the carrier and signed by the customer as proof of delivery (POD). It contains the same information as the bill of lading or the freight bill. Both the carrier and the customer retain a copy. Any damages to the freight should be noted on the D/R.

Bills of Lading

This document is issued by a carrier or shipping department and acknowledges that specific goods have been received on board for shipment. A through bill of lading involves the use of at least two different modes of transport.

Routing

Routes can be chosen manually or with the aid of advanced computer systems that can handle

CHAPTER 8

large volumes of routing data. The basic factors taken into consideration when selecting a route are:

- Distance
- Customer requirements
- Driver availability

Terms To Know

Certificate of Origin
A document attesting to a shipment's country of origin.

Duty (Trade)
A tax levied by government on the importation, exportation, or use and consumption of goods.

Export
Products produced in one country and sold in another.

Free Trade Agreements
An agreement between one or more countries that eliminates tariffs, import quotas, and preferences on most (if not all) goods and services traded between them.

Import
Products bought in one country and produced in another.

Intermodal Transport
1) Shipments moved by different types of equipment combining the best features of each mode.
2) The use of two or more different carrier modes in the through movement of a shipment.

Import Quota
A limit on the quantity of a good that can be produced abroad and sold domestically.

- Vehicle restrictions (For example, some states allow 55 foot trailers and some do not.)
- Highway construction and road closures
- Multiple calls per trip
- Multiple day trip
- Simultaneous delivery and collection options

Regulations
Federal regulations pertain mostly to hazmat transport. However, state governments can regulate which roadways freight carriers can use. States can require carriers to use the National Network of federally maintained highways unless the driver is seeking food, fuel, rest, repairs or to reach a delivery point. Highly populated areas may have time restrictions on when deliveries can be made.

Hazmat Routing
A carrier transporting hazmats must comply with "non-radioactive hazardous material" routes established by federal, state and local governments. Carriers also must route their vehicles away from heavily populated areas, places where crowds assemble, tunnels, narrow streets and alleys.

Tracking Cargo Movement

Yard Management Systems
Keeping track of containers and trailers is an important factor in keeping down costs. A lost or detained container can bear significant costs in detention fees or even lost business if it is a chronic problem. Yard tracking and management systems can be manual or computer-based depending on the size of the yard and volume of traffic. The main objectives of a good yard management system are to monitor and control the traffic as it arrives, is loaded or unloaded and as it leaves.

A yard management system:

- Assists in scheduling and directing a steady flow of traffic into and out of the yard

- Documents the activities and locations of shipments and vehicles

- Coordinates vehicle arrival in staging areas

- Enhances security and accountability

- Reduces detention time and costs

Tracking Systems

Shipments must also be tracked during transport to ensure that they arrive on time and at the right location. When a carrier accepts the shipment, the shipper receives a tracking number. This number is attached to the package or container and allows the shipper and the carrier to follow its progress throughout shipment. The customer usually receives the tracking information as well. This can be entered manually on a written document or into a computer. It can also be an automated process using bar codes or RFID tags to scan the items and record their carrier location and destination.

The ability to automatically identify, track and communicate with stationary and in-transit vehicles and containers is a critical enabler in support of real-time shipment tracking. The use of RFID (Radio Frequency Identification) tags combined with satellite technology allows packages to be tracked in real-time throughout transport.

On-board vehicle communications allow drivers to provide in real time status reports, route changes or delays. This can be done via relayed CB communications, cell phones or more advanced technologies that include cabs equipped with on-board computers connected to headquarters by satellite.

Intermodal Transportation

Intermodal transportation is the movement of goods in one and the same loading unit or vehicle, which uses successively several multiple modes of transport without handling of the goods themselves in changing modes. The introduction of standardized containers and pallets allows for quick transfer of loads between modes of transport with little personnel required.

Intermodal Containers

ISO Containers

ISO has standardized container size and design to allow for the widest possible use of this equipment around the world. The containers are usually large rectangular boxes suitable for ship, rail and truck. They are made of steel and can have open or closed tops or be refrigerated if necessary. The height and width dimensions of the containers are constant, but they can vary in lengths of 20 feet, 40 feet and 53 feet. Container ship capacities are often defined by their ISO container capacities using twenty feet equivalent units (TEU) or forty feet equivalent units (FEU). For example, a ship may be described as being able to carry 3,000 FEU, meaning it could carry 3,000, 40-feet containers or 6,000, 20-feet containers.

CHAPTER 8

Swap-body

This container is used primarily in road and rail modes of transport that conform to different international standards. The container is transferred from truck to rail by an overhead crane.

Unaccompanied Trailers

These are semi-trailers which can be used on ferries or piggybacked onto another trailer for rail transport. This method requires no adaptation of the trailer and does not require personnel to accompany the unit.

Roadrailers

Roadrailers are semi-trailers that are specially designed to run on rails. The road wheels of the trailer can be retracted and a railway bogie attached under the rear of the trailer.

Terms To Know

Shipping Manifest

A document that lists the pieces in a shipment. A manifest usually covers an entire load regardless of whether the load is to be delivered to a single destination or to many destinations. Manifest usually list the items, piece count, total weight, and the destination name and address for each destination in the load.

Shipping Order

A document that specifies the products to be shipped, customer information and the mode of transport

Tariff

An official schedule of taxes and fees imposed by a country on imports or exports.

Intermodal Handling Equipment

Gantry Crane

Also called a straddle carrier, the gantry crane is used to lift containers and swap-bodies. It straddles the containers to quickly move trailers between road and rail vehicles.

Grappler Lift

A grappler lift is similar to a gantry crane but specially fitted to handle swap bodies. It straddles the vehicle and hoists the swap-body.

Reach Stacker

This is a heavy-duty truck used to transfer containers to and from road and rail vehicles or to stack containers on top of each other.

Transtainers

These are used to transfer containers from sea vessels to road or rail vehicles. They are mounted on rails so they can move up and down the dock and have a large boom that can reach onto the ship from the dock.

Intermodal Road Vehicles

Skeletal Trailer

This is a semi-trailer designed to carry ISO containers.

It is fitted with locks at various points on the trailer to allow the vehicle to carry different sized containers. It is called a skeletal trailer because it does not have a loading platform. It is just a framework designed to support the containers it carries.

Extendable Trailers

These are skeletal trailers that can be shortened or extended depending on the size of the container they need to carry.

Intermodal Water Transport Vehicles

Cellular container ship

A specially designed vessel that holds ISO containers stacked on top of one another for maximum capacity filling.

Roll-on Roll-off ferry (RO-RO)

This is a ferry designed to carry road or rail vehicles.

River Barges

Barges can be RO-RO equipped or container ships. They are slow moving vessels that are only used for shipments without time constraints.

Intermodal Rail Vehicles

Rolling Motor Way

This is the rail version of the RO-RO ferry. Entire trucks can be driven onto rail wagons.

Double stacking

In the United States and some other countries, containers may be double stacked and carried by rail.

Customs

Due to the global nature of the supply chain, logistics workers need to be able to work within an international environment. Sale of goods and shipments between countries are controlled by many regulations, agreements and tariffs. While it is not necessary for frontline workers to have an in-depth knowledge of these rules, it is important to have a basic understanding of the terminology used and general operations within the global environment.

Basic Terminology

• Exports are products produced in one country and sold in a foreign country. A U.S. export might be a toolbox that is made in the United States and sold in Mexico.

• Imports are products which have been produced in a foreign country to be sold in this country. A U.S. import might be a car that is made in Germany and sold in the United States.

CHAPTER 8

- Duties and tariffs are taxes imposed by the government on imports and exports.

- Quotas are means of protecting domestic industries by restricting the amount of goods that can be imported during a specific time period.

Governing Bodies

International trade is the exchange of goods and services across national borders. Each country has customs and trade authorities that govern the flow of goods into and out of the country. The United States has several agencies or departments that govern how companies may trade with other countries.

Did You Know?

The United States is the world's second largest exporter with over $2.1 trillion worth of goods in 2021. And it is the world's largest importer, importing more than $2.9 trillion worth of goods that same year.

Imports by the U.S. increased more than 22% since 2017. With a population of 330 million people, the U.S. imports $8,900 a year of product for each resident.

The U.S. is also a member of international agencies that set global standards.

- U.S. Customs and Border Protection (Customs) is part of the Department of Homeland Security and is responsible for enforcing laws with regard to both incoming and outgoing cargo. Customs is also the agency responsible for collecting tariffs (taxes) on imported and exported goods.

- The U.S. State Department (State) regulates the trade of firearms and munitions.

- The Drug Enforcement Agency (DEA) enforces controlled substances laws and works to reduce international illicit drug trade.

- The Food and Drug Administration (FDA) regulates the import of food, pharmaceuticals, animal feed and cosmetics into the U.S. to ensure the health and safety of the general population.

- The World Trade Organization (WTO) is the international organization that supervises world trade. It is responsible for negotiating trade agreements between countries. It has 164 member countries that represent 95% of total world trade.

Trade Regulations

The government regulates trade for many reasons including safety, protecting domestic industry and ensuring a free and competitive national economy. In addition to duties, tariffs and quotas, the following are some important U.S. trade regulations:

- International Traffic in Arms Regulations (ITAR) regulates the exportation of items with specific military application such as firearms, explosives and certain chemicals.

- Container Security Initiative (CSI) regulates U.S. imports by screening containers before they leave foreign ports.

- Advanced Manifest Regulations. Customs requires both importers and exporters to submit electronic notification of shipments in advance.

Free Trade Agreements

Free trade agreements are accords between one or more countries in which they agree to remove barriers to trade by eliminating or reducing tariffs, quotas and other government restrictions. An example is the North American Free Trade Agreement (NAFTA) between the United States, Canada and Mexico that originally went into effect in 1994 and was updated in 2018 that removed most barriers to trade between these three countries.

Customs Documentation

In addition to regular shipping documentation, there are also special documents required when shipping or receiving items internationally.

Commercial Invoice

For international shipments, invoices must often contain port of entry, currency used, country of origin and additional charges or discounts, in addition to other standard invoice information. For imports into the United States, the invoices are also required to be in English.

Import/Export License

The United States does not require a license to import goods (except for a few items). However, the U.S. does require an export license for most exporters of goods.

Certificate of Origin

This is a form provided by the government verifying that the goods being shipped were actually produced in that country. This can become complicated when materials are purchased in one or more countries, assembled in yet another country and are finally imported into the United States. The Generalized System of Preferences (GSP) sets standards for determining the country of origin in those circumstances.

Customs Entry

This is a report filed with customs authorities on imported goods. The complexity of this filing leads many companies to hire special customs brokers to handle the paperwork for them.

Insurance Document

If an exporter is required to insure a shipment, a certificate of insurance must be included with the shipment.

CHAPTER 9

CHAPTER 9

Measuring Weight & Volume

Overview of Chapter

The purpose of this chapter is to explain basic measurements and measurement conversions used in logistics. Much of the world uses the metric system of measurement, so it is a valuable skill to know how to convert measures between the U.S. system and the metric system. This chapter will provide metric conversion tables and explain how to use them.

Objectives

When you have completed this chapter, you will be able to do these things:

1. Calculate basic weight and volume.

2. Convert U.S. measurements to metric.

3. Convert metric to U.S. measurements.

In order to determine the best way to handle and ship materials, you often need to know the weight and/or volume of the materials.

Measuring Weight

The weight of materials is significant for both incoming and outgoing shipments for several reasons. Weight measurements are used to ensure:

- That all cartons contain the correct weight (The value of some goods requires warehouses to ensure that there are no concealed shortages in a unitized pallet load)

- That loads are within weight limits for transport

- That pallets and unit loads are within the capacity of storage facility platforms

- Accuracy of received goods (especially food items)

- Correct stacking height limits

A scale is required to determine the weight of an item or package. There are three types of scales found in most warehouses:

Bench Scales. These are similar to bathroom scales or scales used in a doctor's office or at the gym. These scales are usually used for items weighing less than 500 pounds.

Floor Scales. These are high-capacity scales used for larger and heavier items. The most basic floor scale is a platform sitting on the floor. They require lift truck drivers to place the items on the scale. More sophisticated facilities may have the scale recessed into the floor or may have built in ramps that allow the lift truck or pallet to be driven directly onto the scale.

The weight of the forklift must be pre-measured and subtracted from the total weight to obtain the accurate weight of the products.

Counting Scales. This is a more sophisticated scale that counts by determining the average weight of one item. A worker can then place an entire pallet on the scale, and the scale will calculate the total number of items based on the weight per single unit. These are more common when dealing with large quantities of small parts or products.

Simply determining the weight of a product or package has become less important in recent years as many operations have become volume-based rather than weight-based. Recent changes in the way parcel carriers charge for ground freight provide the best example of this shift.

FedEx, UPS and other parcel carriers used to calculate charges for ground freight based on a package's weight. Under this system, however, carriers felt they were undercharging for large, lightweight packages that took up considerable space in their trailers. To solve this problem, all major U.S. parcel carriers changed their pricing to take the volume of a package into account.

Measuring Volume

Volume is the amount of space that an object takes up. The simplest way to determine the volume of a package or carton is to use a tape measure and perform simple arithmetic. More technologically advanced facilities may use cubing or dimensioning equipment to calculate volume automatically.

Manually Calculating Volume
To measure volume without the aid of cubing equipment, you must have a tape measure of some kind. Volume (V) is found by multiplying the height (H) times the width (W) times the length (L) of an object: $V = H \times W \times L$.

Dimensioning Equipment
Cubing equipment uses laser, infrared or ultrasound technology to scan the dimensions of a package and calculate the volume. Similar to weighing a product, the worker just places the item on a platform and the machine does the rest. Some machines work with a conveyor, so objects pass through an arch that instantly takes the volume measurement.

Metric Conversions
In a global supply chain system, workers need to understand the metric system and how to convert from U.S. measurements to metric. This requirement is especially common in preparing material for shipment abroad.

Standard Units of Measure

There are two basic measurement systems.

U.S. System
U.S. customary units or standard units are the primary and most common units of measurement used in the United States. The basic units of measure in this system are inches, pounds and gallons. The system is derived from and similar to the British Imperial System that evolved from the Romans and Anglo-Saxons over many centuries.

Metric System
The Metric System is the common unit of measure in most of the developed world outside of the United States. The basic units of measure in the Metric System are meters, grams and liters. One goal of the Metric System is to have a single unit for any physical quantity; another important goal is to not require conversion factors when making calculations with physical quantities.

CHAPTER 9

The Metric System is decimal based which means that all multiples and submultiples are factors of powers of ten. For example, one centimeter is ten times larger than one millimeter. Fractions of a unit are not used formally.

It is important for workers throughout the supply chain to understand the basic formulas for converting measurements from one system to another. It is important for material handlers to know how to convert both to and from the Metric System for length, weight (mass) and volume (capacity).

Length

The system for measuring length in the U.S. is customarily based on the inch, foot, yard and mile, which are the only four standard length measurements in everyday use. One inch is equal to 25.4 millimeters or 2.54 centimeters. Note again the power of ten, the decimal point

TABLE 1

Box length: How to convert from the U.S. system to the Metric System

Length		
When You know	**Multiply by**	**To Find**
Millimeters (mm)	0.039	inches
Meters (m)	3.28	feet
Meters (m)	1.09	yards
Kilometers (km)	0.621	miles
Area		
Square Millimeters (mm2)	0.0016	square inches (in2)
Square Meters (m2)	10.764	square feet (ft2)
Square Meters (m2)	1.195	square yard (yd2)
Hectares (ha)	2.47	acres (ac)
Square Kilometers (km2)	0.386	square miles

TABLE 2

Box weight: How to convert from the U.S. system to the Metric System

When You know	Multiply by	To Find
Ounce (oz)	28.35	grams (g)
Pounds (lb)	0.454	kilograms (kg)
Short tons (2000lb) (T)	0.907	megagrams (metric tons) (t)
Grams (g)	0.0352	ounce (oz)
Kilograms (kg)	2.203	pounds (lb)
Megagrams (metric tons) (t)	1.103	short tons (2000lb) (T)

moves one place to the left when millimeters are converted to centimeters. **Table 1** shows how to convert from the U.S. system to the Metric System.

Weight

Weight is measured in ounces, pounds and tons (also called short tons). The metric units are grams, kilograms and megagrams (also called metric tons). **Table 2** converts from the U.S. system to Metric System.

Volume

The cubic inch, cubic foot and cubic yard are the U.S. units most commonly used for measuring volume.

Liters and cubic meters are the metric equivalents. In addition, there is one group of units for measuring volumes of liquids, and one for measuring volumes of dry materials. Details are in **Table 3**.

TABLE 3

Measuring volumes of liquids and dry material

When You know	Multiply by	To Find
Fluid Ounces (fl oz)	29.57	milliliters (ml)
Cup (c)	0.236	liters (L)
(liquid) Pint (pt)	0.473	liters (L)
(liquid) Quart (qt)	0.946	liters (L)
(liquid) Gallons (gal)	3.785	liters (L)
Oil Barrel (bbl)	158.987	liters (L)
(dry) pint (pt)	0.550	liters (L)
(dry) Quart (qt)	1.101	liters (L)
(dry) Gallon (gal)	4.404	liters (L)
Peck (pk)	8.809	liters (L)
Bushel (bu)	35.239	liters (L)
Cubic Feet (ft3)	0.028	cubic meters (m3)
Cubic Yards (y3)	0.765	cubic meters (m3)
milliliters (ml)	0.0338	Fluid Ounces (fl oz)
liters (L)	4.237	Cup (c)
liters (L)	2.114	(liquid) Pint (pt)
liters (L)	1.057	(liquid) Quart (qt)
liters (L)	0.264	(liquid) Gallons (gal)
liters (L)	0.0063	Oil Barrel (bbl)
liters (L)	1.818	(dry) pint (pt)
liters (L)	0.9082	(dry) Quart (qt)
liters (L)	0.2271	(dry) Gallon (gal)
liters (L)	0.1135	Peck (pk)
liters (L)	0.0284	Bushel (bu)
cubic meters (m3)	35.714	Cubic Feet (ft3)
cubic meters (m3)	1.307	Cubic Yards (y3)

CHAPTER 9

Additional Measurements and Conversions

In addition to these basic measures, there are two other conversions that may be useful in different industries: temperature and force. **Table 4** converts from U.S. measurements to Metric System.

TABLE 4

Additional measurements and conversions: Converting U.S. measurements to the Metric System

TEMPERATURE		
When You know	**Multiply by**	**To Find**
Fahrenheit (oF)	(F-32) / 1.8	Celsius (oC)
FORCE		
Poundforce (lbf)	4.45	Newtons (N)
Poundforce per square inch (lbf/in2)	6.89	Kilopascals (kPa)
Celsius (oC)	1.8C + 32	Fahrenheit (oF)
Newtons (N)	0.2247	Poundforce (lbf)
Kilopascals (kPa)	0.1451	Poundforce per square inch (lbf/in2)

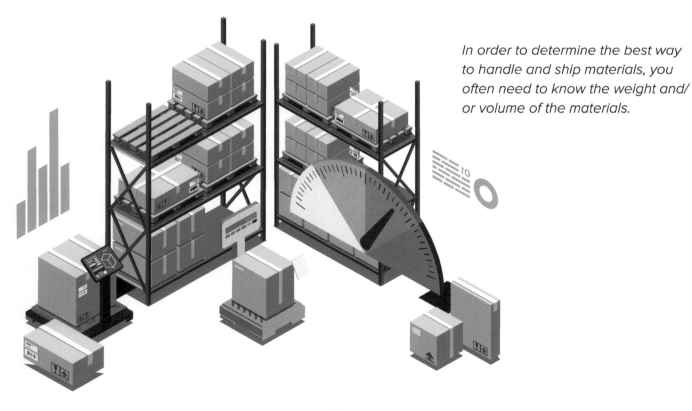

In order to determine the best way to handle and ship materials, you often need to know the weight and/ or volume of the materials.

Notes

Glossary of Terms

Air Waybill
A bill of lading for air transport that serves as a receipt for the shipper, indicates that the carrier has accepted the goods listed, obligates the carrier to carry the consignment to the airport of destination according to specified conditions.

Advanced ship notice (ASN)
An electronic data interchange (EDI) notification of shipment of product.

Aggregate inventory management
Establishing the overall level (dollar value) of inventory desired and implementing controls to achieve this goal.

Automated storage/retrieval system (AS/RS)
A high-density, rack inventory storage system with vehicles automatically loading and unloading the racks.

Batch pick
A method of picking orders in which order requirements are aggregated by product across orders to reduce movement to and from product locations. The aggregated quantities of each product are then transported to a common area where the individual orders are constructed.

Basic description
Required description on documentation when shipping or handling hazmats. It must include: the identification number; proper shipping name; hazard class or division; and packing group (if applicable).

Bill of lading
A carrier's contract and receipt for goods the carrier agrees to transport from one place to another and to deliver to a designated person.

In case of loss, damage, or delay, the bill of lading is the basis for filing freight claims.

Bonding
A system that connects various pieces of conductive equipment together to keep them at the same potential. Static sparking cannot take place between objects that are the same potential.

Cantilever rack
A specialized form of rack used for storing long items such as lumber or pipes.

Carrier freight bill
An invoice presented by the carrier to the shipper, the consignee or a referenced third-party as a demand for payment for services rendered.

Certificate of origin
A document attesting to a shipment's country of origin.

Common carriers
Transportation available to the public that does not provide special treatment to any one party and is regulated as to the rates charged, the liability assumed and the service provided. A common carrier must obtain a certificate of public convenience and necessity from the Federal Trade Commission for interstate traffic.

Consignee
The receiver of shipment of freight; the customer.

Containerization
A shipment method in which commodities are placed in containers, and after initial loading, the commodities per se are not re-handled in shipment until they are unloaded at the destination.

Contract carriers
A carrier that does not serve the general public, but provides transportation for hire for one or a limited number of shippers under a specific contract.

Corrosives
Materials that can attack and chemically destroy exposed body tissues. Corrosives can also damage or even destroy metal. They begin to cause damage as soon as they touch the skin, eyes, respiratory tract, digestive tract, or the metal.

Cross-docking
The concept of packing products on incoming shipments so they can be easily sorted at intermediate warehouses or for outgoing shipments based on final destination. The items are carried from the incoming vehicle docking point to the outgoing vehicle docking point without being stored in inventory at the warehouse. Cross-docking reduces inventory investment and storage space requirements.

Cycle count
An inventory accuracy audit technique where inventory is counted on a cyclic schedule rather than once a year. A cycle inventory count is usually taken on a regular, defined basis (often more frequently for high-value or fast-moving items and less frequently for low-value or slow-moving items). Most effective cycle counting systems require the counting of a certain number of items every workday with each item counted at a prescribed frequency. The key purpose of cycle counting is to identify items in error, thus triggering research, identification, and elimination of the cause of errors.

Decoupling
Creating independence between supply and use of material. Commonly denotes providing inventory between operations so that fluctuations in the production rate of

the supplying operation do not constrain production or use rates of the next operation.

Delivery receipt
A document issued by the carrier that the consignee signs as proof of receipt.

Double-deep storage(also called deep-reach
Rack that holds two units deep, one behind the other.

Drive-in/drive-through rack
High-density storage system that allows units to be stored several deep. Fork trucks can drive between and into racks to retrieve items.

Dunnage
Inexpensive or waste material used to protect and load securing cargo during transport.

Duty (trade)
A tax levied by government on the importation, exportation, or use and consumption of goods.

Exempt carriers
A for-hire carrier that is free from economic regulation.

Export
Products produced in one country and sold in another.

First-in-first-out (FIFO)
A method of inventory valuation for accounting purposes. The accounting assumption is that the oldest inventory (first in) is the first to be used (first out), but there is no necessary relationship with the actual physical movement of specific items.

Fixed costs
An expenditure that does not vary with the production volume; for example, rent, property tax, and salaries of certain personnel.

GLOSSARY

Fixed order quantity ordering
An inventory system, such as economic order quantity, in which the same order quantity is used from order to order. The time between orders (order period) then varies from order to order.

Free trade agreements
An agreement between one or more countries which eliminates tariffs, import quotas, and preferences on most (if not all) goods and services traded between them.

Freight forwarders
The 'middle man' between the carrier and the organization shipping the product. Often combines smaller shipments to take advantage of lower bulk costs.

Full truckload (FTL)
When the load from one customer fills up the whole truck.

Grounding
A special form of bonding in which conductive equipment is connected to an earthing electrode or to the building grounding system to prevent sparking between conductive equipment and grounded structures.

Hazard Communication (HAZCOM)
Also known as the Right-to-Know law. HAZCOM is based on the idea that every worker has the right to know the dangers of the materials they are exposed to at work. The law requires employers to tell employees about the dangers of hazmats and what they can do to protect themselves— before they begin working.

Hazardous material (hazmat)
Hazardous material defined by environmental laws and legal precedents. A product has been defined as hazardous by regulations that impose stiff fines if the regulations are ignored.

Hazmat employee
Any worker who directly affects the safe transportation of hazardous materials.

High-density storage
Storage system that allows pallets to be stored more than one unit deep or high.

Import
Products bought in one country and produced in another.

Intermodal transport

1) Shipments moved by different types of equipment combining the best features of each mode.

2) The use of two or more different carrier modes in the through movement of a shipment.

Import quota
A limit on the quantity of a good that can be produced abroad and sold domestically.

Inventory

1) Those stocks or items used to support production (raw materials and work-in-process items), supporting activities (maintenance, repair, and operating supplies), and customer service (finished goods and spare parts). Demand for inventory may be dependent or independent. Inventory functions are anticipation, hedge, cycle (lot size), fluctuation (safety, buffer or reserve), transportation (pipeline), and service parts.

2) All the money currently tied up in the system. As used in theory of constraints, inventory refers to the equipment, fixtures, buildings, and so forth that the system owns - as well as inventory in the forms of raw materials, work-in-process, and finished goods.

Inventory turnover
The number of times that an inventory cycles, or "turns over," during the year. A frequently used method to compute inventory turnover is to divide the average inventory level into the annual cost of sales. For example, an average inventory of $3 million divided into an annual cost of sales of $21 million means that inventory turned over 7 times.

Item
Any unique manufactured or purchased part, material, intermediate, subassembly, or product.

Just-in-time (JIT)
A philosophy of manufacturing based on planned elimination of all waste and on continual improvement of productivity. It encompasses the successful execution of all manufacturing activities required to produce a final product, from design engineering to delivery, and includes all stages of conversion from raw material onward.

The primary elements of JIT are to have only the required inventory when needed; to improve quality to zero defects; to reduce lead times by reducing setup times, queue lengths, and lot sizes; to incrementally revise the operations themselves; and to accomplish these activities at minimum cost. In the broad sense, it applies to all forms of manufacturing-job shop, process, and repetitive and to many service industries as well.

Kitting
The process through which individual items are grouped or packaged to create a single shipment.

Less than truckload (LTL)
Either a small shipment that does not fill the truck or a shipment of not enough weight to qualify for a truckload quantity (usually set at about 10,000 lbs) rate discount, offered to a general commodity trucker.

Line
A specific physical space for the manufacture of a product that in a flow shop layout is represented by a straight line. In actuality, this may be a series of pieces of equipment connected by piping or conveyor systems.

Material handler
An individual who moves and stages materials within the supply chain.

Materials
For the purpose of this training, materials include other terms such as goods, cargo, freight, loads, products, merchandise, etc.

Material requirements planning (MRP)
A set of techniques that uses bill of material data, inventory data, and the master production schedule to calculate requirements for materials. It makes recommendations to release replenishment orders for material. Further, because it is time-phased, it makes recommendations to reschedule open orders when due dates and need dates are not in phase.

Time- phased MRP begins with the items listed on the MPS and determines (1) the quantity of all components and materials required to fabricate those items and (2) the date that the components and material are required. Time-phased MRP is accomplished by exploding the bill of material, adjusting for inventory quantities on hand or on order, and offsetting the net requirements by the appropriate lead times.

Mobile sliding rack
Storage racks that sit on tracks so they can be moved to retrieve items. An aisle can be opened between any two rows to allow access.

GLOSSARY

Order
A general term that may refer to such diverse items as a purchase order, shop order, customer order, planned order, or schedule.

Order processing
The activity required to administratively process a customer's order and make it ready for shipment or production.

Oxidizer
A substance that oxidizes another substance, especially one that supports the combustion of fuel; an oxidizing agent.

Packaging
The process of using materials to contain and protect a product during handling, storage and shipping

Placard
A poster or sign that measures 10 ¾ x 10 ¾ inches placed on the outside of a container or vehicle to warn that a hazmat is inside the vehicle or container.

Placarding
Use of a poster or sign that measures 10 ¾ x 10 ¾ inches placed on the outside of a container or vehicle to warn that a hazmat is inside the vehicle or container.

POD
Proof of delivery.

Private carriers
A group that provides transportation exclusively within an organization.

Push-back rack
High-density storage system that can hold several units deep on slightly inclined rails. As a unit is removed from the front, the incline causes units behind it to move forward into the front location.

Raw material stock
Purchased items or extracted materials that are converted via the manufacturing process into components and products.

Receiving
The function encompassing the physical receipt of material, the inspection of the shipment for conformance with the purchase order (quantity and damage), the identification and delivery to destination, and the preparation of receiving reports.

Reportable quantity (RQ)
The minimum quantity of a hazardous substance which, if released, is required to be reported.

Reverse logistics
A complete supply chain dedicated to the reverse flow of products and materials for the purpose of returns, repair, remanufacture and/or recycling.

Safety Data Sheet (SDS)
A document intended to provide workers and emergency personnel with procedures for handling or working with a substance in a safe manner, and includes information such as physical data (melting point, boiling point, flash point, etc.), toxicity, health effects, first aid, reactivity, storage, disposal, protective equipment, and spill-handling procedures.

Shipping manifest
A document that lists the pieces in a shipment. A manifest usually covers an entire load regardless of whether the load is to be delivered to a single destination or to many destinations. Manifest usually list the items, piece count, total weight, and the destination name and address for each destination in the load.

Shipping order
A document that specifies the products to be shipped, customer information and the mode of transport

Single-deep storage
Rack that holds only one unit deep.

Staging area
Location in a facility where materials are organized. Newly received items can be staged before being placed in a final storage destination or into another container for transport. Inventory items may also be staged before being organized into orders for container loading.

Staging
Pulling material for an order from inventory before the material is required. This action is often taken to identify shortages, but it can lead to increased problems in availability and inventory accuracy.

Stock keeping unit (SKU)
An inventory item. For example, a shirt in six colors and five sizes would represent 30 different SKUs.

Tariff
An official schedule of taxes and fees imposed by a country on imports or exports.

Unitization
In warehousing, the consolidation of several units into larger units to reduce the number of times all units are handled.

Variable costs
An operating cost that varies directly with a change of one unit in the production volume (e.g. direct materials consumed, sales commissions).

Vertical lift module (VLM)
Automated storage and retrieval system that moves units or items between levels in a facility.

Warehouse management system (WMS)
Software that manages all processes and activities in a warehouse. These processes include receiving, picking, and shipping.

Work-in-process (WIP)
A good or goods in various stages of completion throughout the plant, including all material from raw material that has been released for initial processing up to completely processed material awaiting final inspection and acceptance as finished goods inventory. Many accounting systems also include the value of semi-finished stock and components in this category.

Yard
The outdoor area around a dock; can refer to a shipping yard; rail yard or truck yard.

Zone pick
A method of subdividing a picking list by areas within a storeroom for more efficient and rapid order picking. A zone-picked order must be grouped to a single location before delivery or must be delivered to different locations, such as work centers.

Notes